General Editor's Preface

The death of the novel has often been announced, and part of
the secret of its obstinate vitality must be its capacity for growth,
adaptation, self-renewal and even self-transformation: like some
vigorous organism in a speeded-up Darwinian ecosystem, it
adapts itself quickly to a changing world. War and revolution,
economic crisis and social change, radically new ideologies
such as Marxism and Freudianism, have made this century
unprecedented in human history in the speed and extent of
change, but the novel has shown an extraordinary capacity to
find new forms and techniques and to accommodate new ideas
and conceptions of human nature and human experience, and
even to take up new positions on the nature of fiction itself.

In the generations immediately preceding and following 1914,
the novel underwent a radical redefinition of its nature and
possibilities. The present series of monographs is devoted to the
novelists who created the modern novel and to those who, in
their turn, either continued and extended, or reacted against
and rejected, the traditions established during that period of
intense exploration and experiment. It includes a number of
those who lived and wrote in the nineteenth century but whose
innovative contribution to the art of fiction makes it impossible
to ignore them in any account of the origins of the modern novel;
it also includes the so-called 'modernists' and those who in the
mid- and late-twentieth century have emerged as outstanding
practitioners of this genre. The scope is, inevitably, international;
not only, in the migratory and exile-haunted world of our
century, do writers refuse to heed national frontiers – 'English'
literature lays claims to Conrad the Pole, Henry James the
American, and Joyce the Irishman – but geniuses such as
Flaubert, Dostoevski and Kafka have had an influence on the
fiction of many nations.

Each volume in the series is intended to provide an introduction to the fiction of the writer concerned both for those approaching him or her for the first time and for those who are already familiar with some parts of the achievement in question and now wish to place it in the context of the total *oeuvre*. Although essential information relating to the writer's life and times is given, usually in an opening chapter, the approach is primarily critical and the emphasis is not upon 'background' or generalisations but upon close examination of important texts. Where an author is notably prolific, major texts have been selected for detailed attention but an attempt has also been made to convey, more summarily, a sense of the nature and quality of the author's work as a whole. Those who want to read further will find suggestions in the select bibliography included in each volume. Many novelists are, of course, not only novelists but also poets, essayists, biographers, dramatists, travel writers and so forth; many have practised shorter forms of fiction; and many have written letters or kept diaries that constitute a significant part of their literary output. A brief study cannot hope to deal with all these in detail, but where the shorter fiction and the non-fictional writings, public and private, have an important relationship to the novels, some space has been devoted to them.

To Camilla and Richard Hughes

1
A Writer's Life

Muriel Spark was born Muriel Sarah Camberg in Edinburgh in 1918. Her father was a Jewish engineer whose parents had settled in Scotland, her mother a Gentile who came from Hertfordshire. As a child Muriel Spark went south to spend holidays with her maternal grandmother, who kept a small shop in Watford, portrayed in the autobiographical short story 'The Gentile Jewesses': this grandmother was a colourful personality who had been a suffragette and provided a model for Louisa Jepp in *The Comforters*. This mixed ancestry has been seen as a vital shaping influence. Alan Massie writes that

> it is Muriel Spark's Jewish-Scottish inheritance and upbringing that makes her the moralist she is. When she steps back and says, this is what you have done with your life, this is how you have denied God, this is how you are cursed; then the message, if not the tone, is that of an Old Testament prophet or Calvinist preacher. It is her Jewish-Scottish heritage that allows her to combine a sense of the moral responsibility of action with the determinism that says, "What you have done has unavoidably, unalterably shaped your life."[1]

Massie argues that the remarkable series of novellas that begins with *The Public Image* (1968) 'contrive to effect a synthesis between apparently arbitrary, wilful, undirected behaviour and the working-out of a remorseless inevitable causality' – a long-term legacy of her Scottish childhood and her early exposure to the tenets of Calvinism.

Muriel Spark attended James Gillespie's School for Girls in Edinburgh, and her schooldays there were drawn on in writing *The Prime of Miss Jean Brodie*. Of the Scottish capital itself Muriel Spark has written:

1

Edinburgh is the place that I, a constitutional exile, am essentially exiled from. I spent the first 18 years of my life, during the 1920s and 1930s there. It was Edinburgh that bred within me the conditions of exiledom; and what have I been doing since then but moving from exile into exile? It has ceased to be a fate, it has become a calling.

. . . it is the place where I was first understood. James Gillespie's Girls' School, set in solid state among the green meadows, showed an energetic faith in my literary life. I was the school's Poet and Dreamer, with appropriate perquisites and concessions. I took this for granted, and have never since quite accustomed myself to the world's indifference to art and the process of art, and to the special needs of the artist.[2]

Her exile from Edinburgh began early, for soon after leaving school she married and went to Rhodesia, where her son Robin was born in 1938. Africa is the setting for some of her short stories, and it seems likely that, for instance, 'The Go-away Bird' and 'Bang-Bang You're Dead' contain autobiographical elements, as indeed does much of her work. Noting that 'Mrs Spark is intensely reticent, outside her novels, about her life', Ruth Whittaker shrewdly speculates that 'her desire to keep private the story of her life seems related to her thrift as a writer. She gives the impression of being anxious not to dissipate her material; of hoarding it, with a novelist's awareness of its potential, and ultimately refining it through the alchemic process of her art'.[3]

The outbreak of the Second World War may have prevented her from returning to England; in any case it was 1944 before she was back in London, by which time her marriage had come to an end. In the later stages of the war she was employed on intelligence work in the Political Intelligence Department of the Foreign Office based at Woburn Abbey in Bedfordshire. According to Derek Stanford,

Part of her work was the distortion of news, slanted for German consumption, so as to undermine morale. One such report put out by her team was the story that Hitler had had his pants burnt off him when the bomb exploded in the Generals' plot. This item, I feel, had the true Sparkian touch.[4]

For a year or two after the end of the war she worked as a journalist and in other jobs. In 1947 she met the critic and editor Derek Stanford, whose memoirs provide a vivid and sometimes racy account of her life during the next few years.

In April 1947 Muriel Spark became the General Secretary of the Poetry Society, based in London, and shortly afterwards added to her duties that of editing the Society's journal, the *Poetry Review*. The job brought her more closely in touch with the literary life of postwar London, and some of her novels (especially *Loitering with Intent* and *A Far Cry from Kensington*) reflect this period of her life. After about two years her work for the Poetry Society came to an end after what Stanford refers to as 'a stormy Annual General meeting'[5] at which part of the burden of complaint seems to have been that the General Secretary ventured to pay contributors to the *Review*. At this time, according to Stanford, 'Her reading was individual, thoughtful and assimilated, rather than extensive':[6] her literary interests included the Bible (especially the Old Testament) and the Border Ballads; the influence of both of these can be discerned in her work, her long-standing interest in the Book of Job being most clearly manifested in *The Only Problem*, while her novellas often seem to emulate the narrative economy and dramatic abruptness of the traditional ballads. She also read and translated the Latin lyric poets Horace and Catullus. At this time she 'admitted to no religious beliefs, and did not show much interest in such matters'.[7] When Stanford first met her, she 'blithely called herself a pagan'.[8]

Jobless for a time after leaving the Poetry Society, she lived in the St John's Wood home of Christmas Humphreys, a distinguished lawyer and the leading British Buddhist. She worked briefly for a publicity agent, and started a little magazine, *Forum*, which issued only two numbers. In the early 1950s her first book-length publications appeared: an edited collection of essays on Wordsworth to commemorate the centenary of his death, a book on Emily Brontë, a selection of Mary Shelley's letters, and, a little later, a selection of Newman's letters (all four of these jointly with Derek Stanford), and, on her own account, studies of Mary Shelley and John Masefield and selections of the Brontë letters and of Emily Brontë's poems. Some of these are lightweight literary labours intended to serve an obvious commercial purpose, but a strong interest in women writers is evident. There are also, among much that is fairly routine, from time to time some characteristically original and penetrating observations, as in the following from the Emily Brontë book:

> All great genius attracts legend to itself. Legend is the common means of expressing the manifestation of genius in certain people, who cannot be described in ordinary terms. For this reason the legendary data which adhere to people of genius should be respected. . . . Such legend is the repository of a vital aspect of truth. . . .[9]

The most significant publication of this period, however, is a slim volume of poems, *The Fanfarlo and Other Verse* (1952).

During these years Muriel Spark lived first at Vicarage Gate, off Kensington Church Street in west London, later in the Old Brompton Road in South Kensington, and later still in Queen's Gate Terrace nearby. This is the area in which several of her novels were to be set – an area of wide streets and stately public buildings (the Albert Hall, the Brompton Oratory), and of dignified and spacious houses built for large Victorian and Edwardian families with troops of servants but now divided into small flats and bed-sitting-rooms and occupied by middle-class 'bachelors' of both sexes.

In 1951 she entered and won a Christmas competition for a short story organised by the *Observer* newspaper; the story was 'The Seraph and the Zambesi', which combines, as Derek Stanford says, 'her recent reading of Baudelaire's story *The Fanfarlo* with her own war-time experience of South Africa'. The story is strikingly original and, according to Stanford,

> some readers even wrote to the paper protesting about it receiving the prize. But Mr. Philip Toynbee and Sir Harold Nicolson, who had been among the judges, were enthusiastic. In fact, the Hon. David Astor, Editor of the *Observer*, was so impressed by the story that he turned up at the door of her flat about 2 a.m. on Sunday morning with the first copy of the paper – still wet with news-print – in his hand.[10]

Even its title hints at an important element in the fiction that still lies well in the future: the combination of realistic, precisely localised, even autobiographical, elements with the fantastic and the supernatural.

With Stanford she began to read the works of John Henry Newman (1801–90); at first 'Muriel was won to Newman as much by his style and personality as by the exact sequence of his thought' (Stanford),[11] but in the event she was to follow the religious route Newman had travelled a century earlier, via High Anglicanism to Roman Catholicism. In an important essay, 'My Conversion', published in 1961, she looks back at these crucial years – the years that immediately preceded her flowering as a creative artist – but first describes the background of her early years, religious in spirit if not in observances:

I was born in a very peculiar environment which is difficult to locate. I am partly of Jewish origin, so my environment had a kind of Jewish tinge but without any formal instruction. My schooling was Presbyterian, but I had no definite clear beliefs at all up to 1952. I was terribly interested in the scriptures, but I never went to a Presbyterian church except perhaps for a special service. I was not brought up in any church-going environment, although my parents were really religious and believed in the Almighty. I think I had strong religious feelings as a child which were really bound up with art and poetry, although Christ was a romantic, moving figure. But between my schooldays and 1951, I was almost completely indifferent.[12]

She adds that Newman was 'a tremendous influence' and that she 'tried the Church of England first' before becoming a Catholic. She was baptised into the Church of England by the Rev. C. O. Rhodes, a former editor of the *Church of England Newspaper*, at St Bride's Church, off Fleet Street, and confirmed by the Anglo-Catholic Bishop of Kensington. This Anglo-Catholic period lasted for some nine months from the end of 1953, and for a time she attended services at St Stephen's in Gloucester Road, where T. S. Eliot was also a worshipper.

Before being received into the Catholic Church in 1954, she received instruction from a Benedictine monk, Father Agius of Ealing Priory; and Stanford has recounted how, at this time of her life, she began to experience a number of hallucinations. She believed that T. S. Eliot had broken into her flat and taken items from her food cupboard; that there was a Greek text underlying Eliot's plays, to be arrived at only by some special phonetic pronunciation of the lines in English; and that the blurb in certain of Faber's children's books contained a personal message from the wily Possum to herself. In actual fact, she was suffering from the same condition as Evelyn Waugh had experienced when writing *The Ordeal of Gilbert Pinfold*, a book which came out in the same year (1957) as her first novel *The Comforters*. Both of them were taking pills, prescribed medically, but possibly not according to the doctor's strict instructions. In Muriel's case it was no more than a simple slimming remedy, the trouble probably starting from the fact that she was neglecting herself at the time, eating very little and living largely on excessive potations of tea and coffee.[13]

Muriel Spark's own account in 'My Conversion' suggests that the causes of the hallucinations may have been more complex: she was, she says, 'ready for a breakdown. I think it was the religious upheaval and the fact I had been trying to write and couldn't manage it. I was living in very poor circumstances and I was a bit undernourished as well. I suppose it all combined to give me my breakdown'. She adds that she 'had a feeling while I was undergoing this real emotional suffering that it was all part of the conversion', and that she believes 'there is a connection between my writing and my conversion. . . . Certainly all my best work has come since then'.[14]

She was received into the Roman Catholic Church in 1954 by Father Philip Caraman of the Jesuit Church in Farm Street, and was given psychotherapy by Father O'Malley, Rector of St Etheldreda's, who suggested a rest and a change and prescribed a period of country life. This led her to spend some time at Aylesford Priory, a Carmelite house in Kent which had guest rooms and facilities for retreats, and the short story 'Come Along, Marjorie', set in 'Watling Abbey' in which most of the residents are 'recovering from nerves', seems to refer to this period. The hallucinations themselves play an important part in the experience of the heroine of Muriel Spark's first novel, *The Comforters*, and she shows elsewhere an interest in disembodied voices (for example, the anonymous telephone calls of *Memento Mori*).

'I'm quite sure that my conversion gave me something to work on as a satirist,'[15] Muriel Spark has said, and her career as a creative writer followed this event with remarkable promptness, though it was by a stroke of chance – or the hand of providence – that she was invited at this time to write a novel. The invitation came from the London firm of Macmillan, and the result was *The Comforters*, begun in 1955 and published two years later. 'Writing her novel,' according to Stanford, 'was both therapy and art',[16] and much of it was written in a country cottage in Kent. After returning to London she lived for a time in the suburb of Camberwell, south of the river, which may have provided ideas for the atmosphere of *The Ballad of Peckham Rye*.

Muriel Spark was nearly forty when *The Comforters* appeared, an unusually late start for a novelist, but there is a sense in which her creative life could not begin its most important phase until certain stages in her personal and spiritual life had been passed through. As if to make up for lost time, she proceeded to produce novels at what, even considering their relative brevity, can only be described as an extraordinary rate; but then by this time she not only had a good deal of varied experience to draw upon but had made up her mind on fundamental questions. Of her working methods she has written:

> I like to get my actual writing done quickly. It works up in my head and then the actual physical work of writing takes eight weeks at the most. [Shortly afterwards, however, *The Mandelbaum Gate* was to prove a notable exception to this rule.] With a novel, you know the dialogue. It belongs to each character. But the narrative part – first or third person – belongs to a character as well. I have to decide what the author of the narative is like. It's not me, it's a character.[17]

Some of her remarks in the course of an interview with Frank Kermode also suggest that much of her writing has been done with a kind of single-minded intensity, in a state of almost obsessive preoccupation. She told Kermode that she 'decided that I was writing minor novels deliberately and not major novels':

An awful lot of people are telling me to write big long novels –
Mrs. Tolstoy, you know – and I decided it is no good filling a
little glass with a pint of beer.

KERMODE: You tend to pick not a Tolstoyan society, but a
rather limited society of very old people, for example. Is this
because the other things are on too big a scale for what you
want to do?

SPARK: Well, partly because of my own temperament, and my
own constitution. When I become interested in a subject, say
old age, then the world is peopled for me – just peopled with
them. And it is a narrow little small world, but it's full of old
people, full of whatever I'm studying. They're the center of
the world, and everyone else is on the periphery. It is an
obsession until I've finished writing about them. And that's
how I see things. I wrote a book about bachelors and it seemed
to me that everyone was a bachelor. It is true, just strangely
enough, those people come my way while I am writing – I
don't take a long time, so it is not difficult.[18]

'If I make changes,' she told an interviewer in 1970, 'it's as I go
along, but not afterwards.'[19]

The seven novels from *The Comforters* to *The Girls of Slender
Means*, discussed in the next chapter, had all appeared by 1963.
Not surprisingly, the rate slowed down a little thereafter, and
much more in recent years: after producing seven novels in about
seven years, she has published another eleven in the last 25
years, including three in the last decade. But she must be
regarded, by contemporary standards, as a prolific novelist.

Her early novels achieved a modest critical success, but with
The Prime of Miss Jean Brodie she became a popular, and
commercially a very successful, writer. A number of experiments
in writing radio drama and for the stage were made in the early
1960s. Several of the radio scripts are included in *Voices at Play*
(1961), where the Author's Note states that they were 'written
at the suggestion of Mr. Rayner Heppenstall for the Third
Programme [of the B.B.C.]' and adds: 'I turned my mind into
a wireless set and let the characters play on my ear'. Her play
Doctors of Philosophy was produced in London in 1962. Reviewing
Voices at Play in the *Spectator* (7 July 1961), Evelyn Waugh was
enthusiastic about some of the short stories included in the
volume (he regarded 'Bang-Bang You're Dead' as 'an exquisite

work of art') and declared himself 'proud to have been one of the first of her fellow-writers to spot her', but took a dimmer view of the dramatic experiments. It is difficult not to agree with him, and Muriel Spark has not returned to drama subsequently.

In 1962 she moved to New York, partly in order to escape the pressures of London literary life and the interviews and television appearances that her growing fame threatened to impose upon her (though one might think New York an odd choice of retreat for one seeking peace and quiet). She lived in an apartment close to the United Nations Building and the only important literary outcome of this period is the novel *The Hothouse by the East River*. After about three years she moved again, this time to Italy, where she has lived ever since. Some of her later novels have Italian settings, others reflect in other ways her cosmopolitan, expatriate experience – the state of exile to which she refers in her recollections, already quoted, of her early years in Edinburgh.

2

Angels Dining at the Ritz:
The Early Novels

The Comforters (1957); *Robinson* (1958);
Memento Mori (1959); *The Ballad of Peckham Rye* (1960);
The Bachelors (1960); *The Prime of Miss Jean Brodie* (1961);
The Girls of Slender Means (1963)

Muriel Spark's success in the 1951 *Observer* short story competition did not have the effect of leading her to embrace the art of fiction promptly and wholeheartedly, and it was much later in the decade before she published her first novel. Its composition had begun almost by accident: as already indicated, the suggestion came from the publishing firm of Macmillan, and the advance against royalties enabled her to retire to a country cottage in Kent and to write *The Comforters*. Probably no one could then have guessed either that it would turn out to be the first of seven novels published during a seven-year period, or that thirty years later she would still be writing fiction.

As we have seen, she had at this time been suffering from hallucinations. In an interview first published in 1963 Muriel Spark herself recalled the origins of her first novel:

> I was asked to write a novel, and I didn't think much of novels – I thought it was an inferior way of writing. So I wrote a novel to work out the technique first, to sort of make it all right with myself to write a novel at all. . . .[20]

Interviewees are not upon oath, but there seems to be something unsatisfactory as well as startlingly candid about these statements: to 'make it all right with myself to write a novel at all' seems to go far beyond considerations of 'technique' into the realm of belief and conscience – from 'how' to 'why' and 'whether' – and in *The Comforters* the author seems not only to be exploring the craft of novel-writing but to be trying to define the kind of novel she is prepared to write. Another quotation from the same interview throws some light on this:

> I don't claim that my novels are truth – I claim that they are fiction, out of which a kind of truth emerges. And I keep in my mind specifically that what I am writing is fiction because I am interested in truth – absolute truth. . . .

'A kind of truth', 'absolute truth': these phrases stand in opposition, implicitly, to traditional notions of 'realism' in fiction. If the realism of a novelist such as George Eliot or Zola is 'a kind of truth', it is not Muriel Spark's kind. And here, at the outset, we confront one of the central problems of her art: how can fiction, which is by definition a kind of lying, tell truths? One of the ways is by making no secret of its own fictionality, and this is one of the respects in which *The Comforters* both presages many of its successors and differs from most English novels of its period.

There has been no critical consensus over *The Comforters*, and the unease some critics have felt over it seems to derive from a reluctance to accept that its author is rewriting the rules of the game of fiction. For Patricia Stubbs, Muriel Spark 'effectively hamper[s] her reader's willing suspension of disbelief': it is 'a strange work, chiefly interesting in that it can be regarded as Miss Spark's fictional point of departure, and because it displays, even at this early stage, many of her familiar devices and preoccupations'.[21] Alan Massie finds in it 'an uneasy amalgam of modes'.[22] Against this can be set the enthusiastic response of one of its earliest critics, Evelyn Waugh, who reviewed the novel in the *Spectator* on 22 February 1957. Waugh found it 'intensely interesting', 'highly exhilarating', 'very difficult' but 'rewarding'; with impressive magnanimity he judged this first novel by an almost unknown writer to be more ambitious and more successful than his own novel, *The Ordeal of Gilbert Pinfold*, which appeared in the same year and, like *The Comforters*, dealt with auditory hallucinations. Taking a longer historical view than was available to Waugh, Alan Bold has recently said that 'in the broadly realistic climate of British fiction in the 1950s, *The Comforters* was a strikingly radical book, a flamboyant start to a teasing and powerful fictional career'.[23]

There is a good deal of 'plot' in *The Comforters* – as Waugh observes, it 'thickens to inspissation' – and there is no need here to summarise it in detail. It is worth noting, though, that the main action concerns three women characters: Caroline Rose, Louisa Jepp, and Georgina Hogg. Caroline and Laurence Manders have formerly been lovers, but since her conversion to the Roman Catholic faith they are no more than friends. She is a student of fiction and is writing a book on the form of the novel. As a result of the hallucinations she experiences, she also becomes aware that she is *in* a novel: she hears the tapping of a typewriter and the sound of a voice that utters words taken from the text of the novel we are reading: that is, she is a character in the fiction who at times becomes aware of a world beyond the fiction, the world in which the fiction is being made. (She is the only one who can hear the tapping and the voices, and an attempt to pick them up on a tape-recorder meets with no success.) Another way of putting this is to say that if the novelist, the creator of a work of art, is (as Flaubert said) a kind of God (the Creator), Caroline's awareness of the novel's coming into existence can be compared to her awareness of God's ordering of human affairs, including her own life. She has been seeking God and has also been studying the novel, and her hallucinations bring together the two preoccupations. They are also, of course, preoccupations of Muriel Spark herself.

Mrs Jepp is the grandmother of Laurence Manders and is a robust, almost Dickensian character who lives in the country. Laurence, who is a sports commentator on the radio (another kind of disembodied voice), is also an inveterate snooper, and on his visits to his grandmother discovers that she is involved with a group of diamond smugglers. As for Mrs Hogg, a former employee of the Manders family, she is a Catholic with an urge to secure others for the faith. She has, we learn, no 'private life', and simply disappears when others are not aware of her, first in her own room when she is alone, later in a car in which she is a back-seat passenger. Eventually, after it has been strongly implied that she is a witch, she accidentally drowns after failing to drag Caroline with her under the waters of a river.

Some of the features mentioned above may lead us to treat with scepticism the author's claim that the novel was primarily an exploration of technique, and there are some obvious autobiographical elements, particularly in the presentation of Caroline. She lives in Queen's Gate, South Kensington, a neighbourhood in which Muriel Spark had lived and one to which she returns repeatedly in her novels. Like Muriel Spark, 'She had been in Africa', is a literary critic with a 'literary reputation' (she confesses at one point that in her book *Form in the Modern Novel* she is ' "having difficulty with the chapter on realism" '), and suffers a breakdown. There is a passing reference to 'her family on the Jewish side', and she is evidently a student of the Book of Job, which seems to be responsible for the novel's title (a point pardonably overlooked by Waugh, who remarked, 'I can't think, by the way, why it is called *The Comforters*').

Caroline Rose, who also announces towards the end of the book that she is 'going to write a novel', clearly has much in common with the author. But before we have finished *The Comforters* it becomes clear that it is not enough to talk loosely of an 'autobiographical heroine', for Caroline is presented as the author not just of 'a novel' but of the novel we have been reading. When urged by one of the older characters to ' "Make it a straight old-fashioned story, no modern mystifications. End with the death of the villain and the marriage of the heroine" ', Caroline replies, ' "Yes, it would end that way" ', and that is indeed how *The Comforters* ends. When asked ' "What is the novel to be about?" ' her reply is ' "Characters in a novel" ', and this – fictions within a fiction that constantly draws attention to their and its fictionality – is precisely a description of Muriel Spark's book. There is, finally, an epilogue in which 'the character called Laurence Manders' (the novelistic convention of referring to him as if we were a real person having now been abandoned) is shown 'snooping around in Caroline Rose's flat'. There he finds, as he tells her in a letter, 'an enormous sheaf of your notes for your novel', adding that 'I will tell you what I think of your notes . . . You misrepresent all of us'. Afterwards he destroys the letter without sending it, an act that provokes the final sentence of the novel whose last page we have reached:

He saw the bits of paper come to rest, some on the scrubby ground, some among the deep marsh weeds, and one piece on a thorn-bush; and he did not then foresee his later wonder, with a curious rejoicing, how the letter had got into the book.

It is a conclusion that, in its unexpected lyricism and its hint of what a later novel calls in its closing words 'another world than this', anticipates other conclusions. It is also the point at which the Spark-novel and the Rose-novel at last coincide. The undelivered letter can only have got into 'the book', Caroline's book, by supernatural means. Her book, which is also Muriel Spark's book, has been co-authored by God.

Put thus, in bald terms that possess none of the delicacy or subtlety of the novel-text, the central idea of *The Comforters* may seem merely whimsical – an impression that does much less than justice to the author's deeply serious interest in the relationship between the art of fiction and God's created world. Caroline, a character in a novel, makes notes for a novel (and finally writes it) that includes the characters of Muriel Spark's novel and ultimately turns out to be that novel. But the novelist, or any artist, as creator is only a shadow or imitator of the Creator, and in some sense we are all 'characters' in a 'novel' plotted and written by God. If the novelist is, in Flaubertian phrase, like God in the universe, God is a kind of novelist, planning and plotting, determining ends, doling out rewards and punishments. Just as Caroline hears the voice of the novel's narrator, we too, living in the world that is 'God's novel', may at times become aware of God the novelist at work.

This, or something like it, may be the 'transcendental' meaning of Muriel Spark's first novel, but it is important to remember that it also has an 'aesthetic' dimension in its exploration of the novelist's relationship with her characters and with the story of their 'lives'. None of this, however, has much in common with the realistic and sociological traditions that have been dominant in English fiction from the time of Defoe to Muriel Spark's own contemporaries in the 1950s (the successful novels of the decade include C. P. Snow's *The Masters* (1951), Angus Wilson's *Hemlock and After* (1952), John Wain's *Hurry on Down* (1953), Kingsley Amis's *Lucky Jim* (1954), John Braine's *Room at the Top* (1957) and Alan Sillitoe's *Saturday Night and Sunday Morning* (1958)). *The Comforters* marks a radical break with the dominant fictional tradition, and in it the author makes clear, once and for all, the limitations of her interest in formal realism, in psychological exploration of human character and behaviour, or in consistency of tone. What interests her is in exploring the nature of the novel and of the kind of truth it is capable of telling – and of the relationship of that kind of truth to other kinds.

If this is accepted, some of the criticisms already cited can be seen to be beside the point. It is true that some of the characters are stereotypes or grotesques (the émigré 'Baron', the grandmother-cum-diamond-smuggler), but this is only important in relation to notions of 'character' that Muriel Spark has discarded. It is also true that the novel embodies an 'amalgam of modes', a kind of generic instability, but this is only a fault if measured against a purity of conventions that this author, at least in her early novels, never espouses. The reader's willing suspension of disbelief is not hampered because it is never demanded. We make a mistake if we think of *The Comforters*, and many of this author's other novels, as belonging to the same category as *Emma* or *Middlemarch*, or even *Sons and Lovers* or *Mrs. Dalloway*; it is much closer to *The Pilgrim's Progress* or *A Christmas Carol* or *The Magic Flute*, or to the novels by Hogg and Beerbohm discussed elsewhere in this study. Some of Muriel Spark's critics remind one of the bishop who, after reading *Gulliver's Travels*, declared that he didn't believe a word of it.

In her work 'belief' and 'disbelief', in the sense in which these words are ordinarily applied to fiction (as when we speak loosely of a 'credible' or 'convincing' character), do not arise as issues: she is too interested in what are to her much more important kinds of belief or faith to have much time for what is, after all, not much more than a kind of linguistic evasion (there is a paradox or an evasion in describing as 'credible' a character we know to be invented, and our language, as in using 'character' of both real and fictitious persons, conspires in this laziness or dishonesty). Part of the trouble arises, of course, because a book such as *The Comforters* does not have the kind of purity that we find in, say, *The Faerie Queene* or *Animal Farm*: there are characters, episodes and conversations that would not be out of place in a traditional novel, existing alongside others that seem to belong to some non-realistic genre such as the fairy tale or the ghost story. Like her contemporary William Golding, Muriel Spark shows much less interest in the psychological or sociological novel than in the form's capacity to explore theological, metaphysical or mythic elements; unlike the early Golding of *Lord of the Flies*,

Pincher Martin and *The Inheritors*, however, *The Comforters* and most of its successors effect a compromise between realism and non-realism, placing their fables in commonplace, even banal, settings of place and period.

We perhaps need not take too literally Muriel Spark's account of the origin of her first novel as a groping, hit-and-miss attempt to find out how to write a novel. For a first novel it shows confidence, aplomb, and a clear sense of where she and it are going; the fact that it anticipates many features of her subsequent books suggests that it is anything but a false start. Most novelists writing in England in the 1950s wrote traditional kinds of fiction (Golding is a notable exception); many of them indeed wrote as if the Modernists had never lived. (Things were different in France, where the 'new novel' enjoyed a considerable vogue and expressed its discontent with the persistence of traditional modes of fiction. Alain Robbe-Grillet's *Pour un nouveau roman* appeared in 1963 and was translated as *Towards a New Novel* in 1965.) The striking quality of *The Comforters* is the firmness with which it severs connections with the past and frustrates realistic and mimetic expectations. Rather than being an imitation of other novels it is a novel about the novel that enlarges from the aesthetic to the theological, taking the act of writing a novel as a paradigm for the workings of God's purposes in the world. From the moment in Chapter 5 when Caroline tells Laurence of 'her theory about the author making a book out of their lives', the parallel or parable is frequently brought to the reader's attention (see, for example, pp. 95, 97, 101, 103–5, 160–2, 167, 181 in the Penguin edition).

The Comforters illustrates Malcolm Bradbury's statement that 'Among the recurrent themes and modes of [Muriel Spark's] work has long been a curiosity about the relation of an author to a fiction and its agents'.[24] Another critic, Frank Kermode, remarks of a much later novel, *The Driver's Seat*, that Mrs Spark is there 'a writer growing more and more parsimonious in the provision of interpretative handouts'.[25] It is not a complaint that can be brought against *The Comforters*, where the transcendental impinges frequently upon the material, and with increasing frequency as we read on. The much sparer and austerer art of *The Driver's Seat* and the later work in general is still a long way ahead. But this first novel is anything but transparent, and, as the verdicts of even recent critics suggest, retains its power to tease and perplex.

In *Robinson*, published in the following year, Muriel Spark turned to the first-person narrative method, an experiment she was not to repeat until *Loitering with Intent* more than twenty years later. Despite this technical difference, there is an obvious resemblance between Caroline Rose in *The Comforters* and the heroine of this second novel, January Marlow, who is a young poet, critic and journalist, a Catholic convert, a widow (after a brief marriage), and a confident woman of independent outlook. The autobiographical elements in this portrait are hard to ignore, and such a reading seems almost to be encouraged by the private jokes dropped into the text (references to Derek Stanford and to the author herself) and in its very title (Muriel Spark's only son is named Robin).

On a business flight to the Azores, January is involved in a plane crash and, with two other survivors, finds herself on a tiny island named Robinson after the recluse who has settled there and for whom the arrival of these unexpected visitors is anything but welcome. This situation, and the map that prefaces the narrative (as in *Gulliver's Travels* and *Treasure Island*), suggest at once that this will be a reworking, or perhaps a parody, of the kind of island story that has been a popular form of fiction since Defoe's *Robinson Crusoe*, the imitations of which are collectively known as 'Robinsonnades'. Four years before *Robinson*, William Golding had scored a considerable success with his first novel, *Lord of the Flies*, an island story with strong theological overtones, and it seems very likely that Muriel Spark's choice of a theme may have been to some degree influenced by this book. As in Golding's novel, the small society of the island generates not comradeship and co-operation, but hostility, fear, suspicion, and eventually violence.

The island itself is strikingly and implausibly man shaped, and although there is a good deal of detailed realistic description of its features it is also, as Alan Bold has shown, a carefully worked-out exercise in symbolism:

> Held east-upmost, the map of Robinson resembles a human shape, with the Headlands as head, the North and South Arms as upper extremities, the North and West Leg as lower limbs. Looked at cartographically Robinson's nineteenth-century Spanish-style stone bungalow, on a plateau a thousand feet above sea-level, is located at the navel of the island. There

is a secret tunnel at the heart and a live crater, the Furnace, at the liver. The absence of any obvious anatomical landmark at the crotch of the island, situated vulnerably at Shark Bay, has sexual connotations in an allegorical context.[26]

Here the contemporary castaways must remain until, in some three months' time, a boat makes its annual visit to the island to collect the pomegranate harvest. (Although telling an allegorical tale in a symbolic setting, Muriel Spark is, as so often, carefully precise about the time scheme: as the opening page of the novel tells us, January has 'not been ten days on the island' when she begins the journal that forms the basis of her narrative and bears the starting date 'May 20, 1954'; it may be just coincidence that the year is that of the publication of *Lord of the Flies*.) The three visitors stranded for three months are examples of what Peter Kemp nicely calls the 'insistent trios'[27] of this novel: January is the only woman in the company of three men, she is one of three sisters, and she is writing a book about three islands for a series dealing with 'threes of everything'. This is by no means the last time that Muriel Spark will show a fascination with numerology, and here the relevance seems to be to the doctrine of the Trinity. The most dramatic event in the novel, Robinson's disappearance and presumed murder, occurs on 3 July.

Robinson himself has trained for the Catholic priesthood but has withdrawn at a late stage on account of his conviction that the Church has fallen into heresy in its worship of the Virgin Mary; he has written a book, *The Dangers of Marian Doctrine*. Ironically and unhappily, his own middle name is Mary. Ruth Whittaker's persuasive reading of this element in the novel stresses the aridity of Robinson's intellectual approach to his faith, as contrasted with the more instinctive (and specifically feminine) attitude of January:

In *Robinson* the heroine progresses, as it were, to realising the dangers of a purely intellectual approach to Catholicism, which Mrs Spark implies is one sort of denial of faith. Significantly, Robinson ... cultivates only the headlands, ignoring the potential fertility of the rest of [the island], and living mainly on imported food from tins. The cultivation of the intellect at the expense of the instincts is a source of disquiet to January, and she begins to reject the repressive function that Robinson represents.[28]

The secular counterpart of Robinson's hostility to Mariolatry is his misogyny, and specifically his attitude towards January Marlow. In his self-absorption he anticipates the murderous solipsist Patrick Seton in *The Bachelors*, just as Seton's fraudulent spiritualism is anticipated by Tom Wells's trading in the occult. Muriel Spark tends to repeat character types with variations, so that a figure in one novel appears like a sketch for a later one. She is also much preoccupied by quasi-religious beliefs and practices, shabby or dishonest substitutes for real faith.

The motif of the man-shaped island is extended into a frequent identification of persons and places – Robinson, Marlow, Wells and Waterford are all place-names as well as names of characters in the book – and reaches its climax in the quoting of Donne's famous declaration that 'no man is an island'. In retreating from the world Robinson has sought to turn himself into an island, cutting himself off from the human community and merging his identity with that of the island that bears his name. But Robinson is not unique, for the ill-assorted trio of visitors to his retreat all fail to make connection with each other as well as with him: linked by their common humanity, they find no shared ground of convictions or values that can form a basis for relationships, and Robinson's feigned murder brings their latent antagonisms out into the open.

Critics have detected a continuity between Muriel Spark's first two novels. Alan Bold, for instance, finds both remarkably successful 'as experimental applications of fictional form' and as 'conveying the spiritual isolation of a woman temperamentally tempted to solipsism', while Peter Kemp sees *Robinson* as providing 'a kind of annexe to *The Comforters*': 'Both are books concerned with isolation, but in the second, the emphasis falls more upon the odd connections that, despite this, can exist'.[29] The two critics differ sharply, however, in their evaluation of the novel: for Bold it works as 'a religious allegory', but Kemp judges it too mechanical and even geometrical in conception and structure to be satisfactory. Anticipating a phrase that will be used in *The Prime of Miss Jean Brodie*, Kemp states that

the commonplace is not satisfactorily transfigured; the central situation retains the appearance of an extreme and local coincidence, not something of wider relevance; a convincing image is not created out of the society portrayed. The man-shaped island, which, at first sight, looks the most allegorical of all Mrs Spark's settings, turns out to be the least effectively so.[30]

I would myself want to endorse this judgement: the narrative is uncompelling, and the severe restrictions placed upon setting and characters, though not in themselves (as Golding had shown in *Lord of the Flies*) necessarily inimical to imaginative power or universality, seem to bring in their train a narrowness of vision. Perhaps the most striking implicit comment on *Robinson* is the fact that, in its author's development as a novelist, the island represents a blind alley: it resembles none of the other novels of her early period, and in its immediate successor she was to return to the world of London that had already been explored in *The Comforters*, to a third-person narrative that ranged much more widely than the single view of even a partially autobiographical heroine could do, and to social groups and characters that convey a much stronger sense of human variety and strangeness than the sparsely populated Robinson island could ever provide.

The Latin phrase 'memento mori' means 'remember that you must die' and has traditionally been used to refer to an emblem of mortality such as a skull, serving as a reminder that death awaits us all: Shakespeare, for instance, refers in *Henry IV Part I* to 'a death's head or a memento mori'. The phrase is normally encountered in religious contexts, and despite appearances *Memento Mori* is, as Patricia Stubbs says, 'a religious book'. In Muriel Spark's novel, however, the skull is replaced by a more intrusive and insistent twentieth-century counterpart: a voice, or perhaps several voices, heard over the telephone (further evidence of the fascination with disembodied voices that has already been exhibited in *The Comforters*). Most of the characters in this novel are old, and many of them receive telephone calls reminding them that they must die. Some receive them repeatedly – in the opening lines of the novel Dame Lettie Colston receives her ninth such anonymous message.

Although the message is always the same, the caller's identity and even sex seem to vary; thus Dame Lettie hears a voice that is 'quite cultured' whereas her brother Godfrey's caller is 'a common little fellow, with his lisp'. The possibility is likely to cross the reader's mind that the voices people hear, like the number of calls they receive, indicates something about them rather than about external reality. Yet the calls cannot be dismissed as auditory hallucinations since, unlike the voices heard by Caroline Rose in *The Comforters*, they are sometimes heard by those for whom they are not intended. Different people respond in different ways to these unsettling messages, which constitute the familiar fictional and dramatic device of the test or trial. No rational or realistic explanation of them is ever offered, though there is a supernatural explanation that on its own terms is entirely adequate.

One of Muriel Spark's most recent critics, Alan Bold, has characterised *Memento Mori* as 'pessimistic' and 'a macabre melodrama' and has referred to 'its sombre theme of the fatal fragility of old age'.[31] This seems to me both to misrepresent the novel's tone and temper and to misplace its centre of gravity. Although, as Bold points out, its complex plot involves intrigue, blackmail, bigamy, murder, and at the end a catalogue of deaths from a wide variety of the afflictions that flesh is heir to, it is at the same time a very funny book, witty and ironic, stylish and elegant, consistently serious but never 'sombre'. As one of the three epigraphs, a quotation from the *Penny Catechism*, reminds us, Death is the first of 'the four last things to be ever remembered' by a Christian (the others being Judgement, Hell and Heaven). The other two epigraphs form a contrast to each other: W. B. Yeats's cry of indignant protest in his late poem *The Tower* at the 'absurdity' of 'decrepit age', and the intense enthusiasm of the seventeenth-century mystical writer Thomas Traherne, whose childhood vision perceives the aged as 'Venerable and Reverend Creatures . . . Immortal Cherubims!'. (A sentence, not quoted by Muriel Spark, that appears a little later in the same passage from Traherne's *Centuries of Meditations* has a broad relevance to her work as a novelist: 'Eternity was manifest in the Light of Day and something infinite behind everything appeared . . .'.)

Memento Mori presents unflinchingly and unsentimentally 'the fatal fragility of old age' and depicts in full measure what Yeats calls the 'absurdity' of human decline; but to suggest that its main purpose is to present scenes from geriatric life and its main effect to disturb or depress the reader with the prospect of his or her own bodily (and perhaps mental) disintegration is to make it sound like a novel different from, and much less original and interesting than, the one we actually have before us.

A number of contemporary writers have essayed what might be called the geriatric novel: William Trevor in *The Old Boys*, for instance, Paul Scott in *Staying On*, Barbara Pym in *Quartet in Autumn*, and Kingsley Amis in *Ending Up* and *The Old Devils*. Such portrayals, pathetic or macabre or sad or ludicrous, of old age stand in contrast to the preoccupation with youth characteristic of the nineteenth-century novel and exemplified most obviously in the *Bildungsroman* or novel of growth and development (*Jane Eyre, David Copperfield*, etc.). The latter reflects a confidence in the possibility of individual progress and improvement, and often a faith in the workings of Providence, that the late twentieth century has generally been unable to share. Hence, contemporary versions of the *Bildungsroman* such as those of William Golding (*Lord of the Flies, Rites of Passage*) tend to subvert and parody earlier models. The portrayal of old age in the influential novels and plays of Samuel Beckett is disquieting, even repellent – closer to Swift's Struldbrugs in the third book of *Gulliver's Travels* than to the serene and dignified Victorian patriarch, full of years and wisdom.

For Muriel Spark as a Catholic novelist, however, death is not a fearful and sometimes humiliating and painful end, but a beginning; it is also not just an unwelcome epilogue or coda to the real business of living, and one we do our best to put out of our minds, but a fact of life that should inform and irradiate every stage of our existence. The telephone messages in the novel are not just a 'macabre hoax' (in Patricia Stubbs's phrase)[32] but an angelic or divine warning intended for the spiritual good of the recipient; the word 'angel', it is worth recalling, comes from the Greek word for 'messenger'.

The various characters make very different responses to the voice that says simply – but for some unnervingly, producing panic or indignation – 'Remember you must die'. Dame Lettie, like her brother Godfrey, blusters and complains: they 'place' themselves morally as well as socially by treating it as a social nuisance and a personal affront, resort to the police, talk of a letter to *The Times* and 'a question in the House'. Alec Warner, an elderly gerontologist (and hence both investigator and specimen of his own branch of scientific enquiry), is dispassionate and rationalistic, responding to the message by making entries on his file-cards and noting the hypothesis 'mass-hysteria'. Godfrey's wife Charmian, a former popular novelist who is near senility in the early part of the story but regains a grip on life as it progresses, is a Catholic who shows a calm acceptance of the inevitable:

'Remember,' he said, 'you must die.'

'Oh, as to that,' she said, 'for the past thirty years and more I have thought of it from time to time. My memory is failing in certain respects. I am gone eighty-six. But somehow I do not forget my death, whenever that will be.'

'Delighted to hear it,' he said. 'Good-bye for now.' (Chapter 10)

The two characters who come closest to solving the puzzle, however – who do in fact solve it in all but realistic and material terms – are not centrally involved in the action but occupy different points on its periphery. Henry Mortimer, a retired detective whose surname suggests a connection with death, is asked to solve the mystery and eventually comes up with a solution that fails to satisfy those who have hoped for the exposure of a malicious hoax and the arrest of an offender:

'And what's the motive?' said Godfrey. 'That's what I ask.'

'The question of motive may prove to be different in each case, to judge by the evidence before us,' said Mortimer. 'I think we must all realize that the offender is in each case whoever we think he is ourselves.'

This 'solution' is offered in a scene in Chapter 11 that seems to be a parody of the familiar 'clearing up' scene in the classic detective story in which the main characters are assembled to hear the detective expound the process by which he has identified the criminal – an example of Muriel Spark's fondness for parodying stock fictional situations, as if to mock the conventions by which fictions habitually conduct their business. (As Caroline Rose remarks in *The Comforters*, '"I haven't been studying novels for three years without knowing some of the technical tricks. In this case it seems to me there's an attempt being made to organize our lives into a convenient slick plot. . . .'": Penguin edition, p. 104.)

A page or two earlier Mortimer has said:

> 'If I had my life over again I should form the habit of nightly composing myself to thoughts of death. I would practise, as it were, the remembrance of death. There is no other practice which so intensifies life. Death, when it approaches, ought not to take one by surprise. It should be part of the full expectancy of life. Without an ever-present sense of death life is insipid. You might as well live on the whites of eggs.'

and this view of death as 'part of the full expectancy of life' suggests that Mortimer is a spokesman for the authorial point of view. It is not, though, a view that is shared by the others who are present: Dame Lettie reiterates her complaints of police inefficiency, Charmian suggests sentimentally that the caller 'may be lonely, and simply wanting to talk to people', Alec clings to his pseudo-scientific theory of mass-hysteria, and so on.

It is Jean Taylor, the least mobile character in the book, who most fully embodies wisdom and an understanding of the meaning of these events. Jean, the former maid and companion to Charmian, is now bedridden and in constant pain, but hearing of the telephone calls only from other characters who visit her in hospital she arrives at an awareness of their significance. Quite early in the book she tries in vain to instruct Dame Lettie in a proper response to the voice on the telephone:

> 'Can you not ignore it, Dame Lettie?'
> 'No, I can not. I have tried, but it troubles me deeply. It is a troublesome remark.'
> 'Perhaps you might obey it,' said Miss Taylor.
> 'What's that you say?'
> 'You might, perhaps, try to remember you must die.'
> She is wandering again, thought Lettie. . . . (Chapter 4)

Later she offers the most explicit interpretation of its meaning:

> 'In my belief,' she said, 'the author of the anonymous telephone calls is Death himself, as you might say. I don't see,

Dame Lettie, what you can do about it. If you don't remember
Death reminds you to do so. . . .' (Chapter 13)

Jean Taylor is the real heroine of the story, a figure of dignity
and fortitude, and of faith undiminished by suffering, 'the only
problem' to which Muriel Spark was to return in one of her late
novels. Like other truth-tellers it is Jean's fate not to be believed
by those who are imprisoned in their own worldly personalities
and convictions, whether self-indulgent, authoritarian or rationalist.

Jean Taylor is a patient in the Maud Long Medical Ward,
and again the name is suggestively symbolic, 'Maud' being
phonetically close to *mors* and *mort*, and 'Maud Long' implying,
relevantly enough, a long dying. The twelve occupants of the
ward, whose number recalls Christ's Apostles, are collectively
known as the Grannies and form a kind of chorus, alternately
grotesque and pathetic, to the main action. These old ladies are
no longer capable of physical action or the exercise of will: the
comic inappropriateness of the horoscopes that one reads aloud
from the newspaper (*'A day for bold measures. . . . A wonderful
period for entertaining. . . .'*) and the frequent threats of another
to change her will merely underline their helplessness. In these
portions of the novel a sense is conveyed of old age as a stage of
life with its own identity, involving a reluctant foray into
alien territory for which previous experience has provided no
preparation:

'It is like wartime,' Miss Taylor remarked.
'What do you say?'
'Being over seventy is like being engaged in a war. All our
friends are going or gone and we survive amongst the dead
and the dying as on a battlefield.'
She is wandering in her mind and becoming morbid, thought
Dame Lettie. (Chapter 4)

And later, as seen by another character:

How primitive, Guy thought, life becomes in old age, when
one may be surrounded by familiar comforts and yet more
vulnerable to the action of nature than any young explorer at

the Pole. And how simply the physical laws assert themselves,
frustrating all one's purposes. (Chapter 14)

In the first of these quotations it is noteworthy that Dame Lettie,
herself an old woman who changes her will out of pique, refuses
to recognise a truth that is among other things a truth about
herself. These are, as often elsewhere, the sheep and the goats
of Muriel Spark's fictional world, those who accept and those
who cannot or will not accept the truth when it is presented to
them.

All in all, *Memento Mori* is not only the best of the author's
first three novels but one of the most satisfying of all her books.
Turning away from the restrictions of cast and setting with
which she had experimented in *Robinson*, she returns in it to the
more crowded and socially varied world of *The Comforters*. As in
that novel, what we may called the worldly plot is complex,
almost a Victorian novel in miniature, with its secrets and
coincidences and its reliance on action, including crime. But the
effect of this is almost parodic, as if the convolutions of traditional
fiction were being held up for amused critical inspection. The
other plot, the supernatural or providential plot of the mysterious
telephone calls and their significance, has an impressive simplicity, that of fable or parable. Appropriately it is Charmian,
whose own fictions are after a period of neglect enjoying a
renewed vogue and being reprinted, who comments that '"the
art of fiction is very like the practice of deception"', adding that
'"In life . . . everything is different. Everything is in the
Providence of God"' (Chapter 14). The tongue-in-cheek summary of one of Charmian's novels (the fictions of a fiction)
suggests that she is a very different kind of novelist from Muriel
Spark, but the comments quoted demand to be taken seriously.
In the fiction titled *Memento Mori* we seem to be presented with
worlds that stand at different distances, or different angles, from
the 'reality' of the world we inhabit daily. What I have called
the 'worldly' plot, allied (even if parodically) to traditions of
fictional realism, is merely 'the practice of deception', like a
conjuring trick; but the 'supernatural' plot, for all its refusal to
make concessions to 'realism', is actually closer to the lives we
live, lives that are 'in the Providence of God'.

As often elsewhere, Muriel Spark's rejection of the mimetic
tradition involves an element of parody that exposes the falsity

of fictions that make untenable claims to represent reality. *Memento Mori* is among other things a parody of the conventional detective story, a genre that emerged at a time of rapidly declining religious faith and one that takes for granted the primacy of our existence in a material universe dominated by the laws of logic. Classic detective fiction, having propounded a puzzle, sets itself the task of finding a solution on the assumption that all questions have answers, and in the process makes much play with the phenomena of the material world: bloodstains, footprints, tobacco ash, and the like. 'Scientific' and 'deduction' are favourite words of that arch-rationalist Sherlock Holmes, who does not seem to have been a churchgoer. In Muriel Spark's novel, on the other hand, there is a mystery but, so far as the official files are concerned, no solution. Since, however, her world is not exclusively or even primarily a material one, Jean Taylor's solution (unlikely candidate though she is for the role of detective) is not only the best we are given but is entirely satisfying, and Death must be numbered among the characters of the novel – as why, indeed, should he not?

It is, finally, Jean Taylor who is the last to be named at the end of a novel preoccupied with endings. Again, the final couple of pages have a parodic flavour: instead of the marryings and begettings, the material and emotional rewards of the traditional novel, there is a catalogue of deaths. It is a case not so much of happy ever after (though some are presumably that) as of exchanging time for eternity. Characteristically, language and tone modulate in the closing sentences: from the vocabulary of the death certificate, the official and worldly reaction to the passing of a soul and the rational concern with causes ('hypostatic pneumonia', 'uraemia', 'carcinoma of the cervix', etc.) there is a shift to the spiritual world of Jean Taylor, who spends her last days 'employing her pain to magnify the Lord, and meditating sometimes confidingly upon Death, the first of the four last things to be ever remembered'.

The Ballad of Peckham Rye, the first of the two novels published by Muriel Spark in 1960, is a less satisfying work than *Memento Mori* but hardly deserves its dismissal by one critic as 'a relative failure'.[33] It is short, giving the impression of being an extended short story; the scale of its setting and action are limited; and its ambitions are much narrower than those of its immediate predecessor. This story of lower-class life in a suburb of south London has a superficial realism that is undercut by the 'ballad' promise of its title and by the anarchic, demonic hero or anti-hero Dougal Douglas. To this extent it is characteristic of Muriel Spark's refusal to play the game of fiction according to the time-honoured rules.

With his Scottish name and his claim to be a graduate of the University of Edinburgh, the figure of Dougal suggests that the kind of ballad in question may be the traditional Border ballad such as 'Sir Patrick Spens' or 'The Demon Lover'. These poems are typically short to the point of being elliptical, show great narrative economy, make use of laconic dialogue and stylised description, and introduce scenes of death and often of violence and the supernatural. They are also transmitted by oral tradition and much modified in the telling. All these qualities are to be found embodied or referred to in the novel, which affirms the connection between its story and the ballad or folktale tradition by drawing attention at the beginning and end to the way in which, even in a twentieth-century urban community, folklore and legend enjoy a vigorous life:

But in any case, within a few weeks, everyone forgot the details. The affair is a legend referred to from time to time in the pubs when the conversation takes a matrimonial turn. Some say the bridegroom came back repentant and married the girl in the end. Some say, no, he married another girl, while the bride married the best man. It is wondered if the bride had been carrying on with the best man for some time past. It is sometimes told that the bride died of grief and the groom shot himself on the Rye. It is generally agreed that he answered 'No' at his wedding. That he went away alone on his wedding day and turned up again later. (Chapter 1)

Some said Humphrey came back and married the girl in the end. Others said, it was like this, Dixie died of a broken heart and he never looked at another girl again. Some thought he had returned, and she had slammed the door in his face and called him a dirty swine, which he was. One or two recalled there had been a fight between Humphrey and Trevor Lomas. But at all events everyone remembered how a man had answered 'No' at his wedding. (Chapter 10)

The one 'event', that 'a man had answered "No" at his wedding' (a kind of parodic inversion of the famous scene in *Jane Eyre*), has given rise to a crowd of inventions; and in relation to the 'real' events of the novel (the second passage quoted above continues 'In fact they got married two months later . . .') these rumours and tales, orally disseminated and incrementally elaborated, stand as fictions. But of course the 'real' events are themselves fictions, and this multiplying or squaring of fictions is by now a Sparkean trademark.

It is to be found again in the figure of Dougal, a fiction who is also, like so many of Muriel Spark's major characters, a maker of fictions, giving different accounts of the same events to different people, assuming the expressions and postures of different personalities (he has been an actor in a student production), even using two names, one a reversal, mirror image or alter ego of the other. As the newcomer or intruder into a settled and ordered society, Dougal performs a familiar novelistic function, and the story traces his impact on certain families and organisations in Peckham from his arrival to his departure. He is an ambiguous and chameleon-like figure whose fictions simultaneously disturb the peace, unsettling the lives of others, and serve his own advancement. He is a persuasive liar who takes on different jobs under different names. And he is also an author, and even a kind of novelist, since one of his enterprises is the ghost-writing of the memoirs of an elderly actress, for whom he invents a Peckham childhood that never existed. It begins to look, therefore, as though this simple story of suburban alarms and excursions, deceptions and confusions, is also a commentary on the nature of fiction and its power to deceive and lead astray.

We know from her earlier work, however, that Muriel Spark's novels are liable to have a theological as well as an aesthetic dimension, and we may at this point recall that not only are fictions another name for lies but the Father of Lies is Satan. And there is certainly something satanic or diabolical about Dougal. Not only, as already noted, is he a tempter and a mischief-maker, a liar and deceiver, and one with the gift (like Milton's Satan) of assuming different guises, but he has two little knobs on his head where horns have been surgically removed. At the end of the book he quits Peckham and is

away off to Africa with the intention of selling tape-recorders to all the witch doctors. 'No medicine man,' Dougal said, 'these days can afford to be without a portable tape-recorder. Without the aid of this modern device, which may be easily concealed in the undergrowth of the jungle, the old tribal authority will rapidly become undermined by the mounting influence of modern scepticism.'

Consistently enough, he will be trading in a form of magic that is also a means of deception. (The paragraph is perhaps also a fond, or a self-mocking, retrospective glance at the author's own first novel, in which a tape-recorder plays a part, and at her third, in which a voice transmitted by another 'modern device' reminds the worldly of 'the old tribal authority', the Church's teaching on preparation for dying.)

Dougal may owe something to a remarkably original, and technically experimental, Scottish novel, James Hogg's *The Private Memoirs and Confessions of a Justified Sinner* (1824). Hogg's sinner is befriended and tempted by a mysterious figure who turns out to be Satan and who possesses the art of appearing in many forms:

> 'I beg your pardon, sir,' said I. 'But surely if you are the young gentleman with whom I spent the hours yesterday, you have the cameleon art of changing your appearance; I never could have recognized you.'
>
> 'My countenance changes with my studies and sensations,' said he. 'It is a natural peculiarity in me, over which I have not full control. If I contemplate a man's features seriously, mine own gradually assume the very same appearance and character. And what is more, by contemplating a face minutely, I not only attain the same likeness, but, with the likeness, I attain the very same ideas as well as the same mode of arranging them, so that, you see, by looking at a person attentively, I by degrees assume his likeness, and by assuming his likeness I attain to the possession of his most secret thoughts. . . .'[34]

This is very close to Dougal's behaviour on his first appearance (Chapter 2), where at one moment he 'changed his shape and became a professor', at another 'leaned forward and became a television interviewer'; in the next chapter he 'gazed at

[Humphrey] like a succubus whose mouth is its eyes' and, walking with a girl in a cemetery, 'posed like an angel on a grave. . . . He posed like an angel-devil . . .'.

All of this makes Allan Massie's comment that Dougal is 'a memorable but not entirely convincing character'[35] distinctly odd. As a criterion, notions of what is 'convincing' seem irrelevant to this tale of the intrusion of demonism into suburban life: one might as well object that the busts of the Roman emperors who register Zuleika Dobson's arrival in Oxford in the opening chapter of Max Beerbohm's novel are not 'convincing'. It is true that Peckham is depicted in a vein of topographical and social authenticity, and that there are many 'period' touches: it is a Fifties world of television and popular songs, and the heroine, Dixie Morse, 'daughter of the first G.I. bride to have departed from Peckham and returned', dances 'to the rhythm of *Pickin' a Chicken*'. But Dougal exists on a different plane and could have had no place in a novel by, say, Arnold Bennett or Henry James, or by one of Muriel Spark's realist contemporaries, though he would have been perfectly at home in a story by Beerbohm or in one of those late Victorian or Edwardian fantasies (E. M. Forster wrote several) in which the god Pan makes his appearance in the English countryside.

Muriel Spark is less interested in 'pure' realism or 'pure' fantasy (*Pride and Prejudice*, say, or *Alice's Adventures in Wonderland*) than in the intersection or blending of the two. And this in turn brings us back to our starting point in the discussion of this novel: the explicit association with the popular ballad, which can mingle stark realism and even a relationship to history with fantasy and the supernatural. (One of Muriel Spark's early poems is titled 'The Ballad of the Fanfarlo' and adopts the traditional ballad stanza-form.) And in the end even the realistic elements in the book reveal their instability and threaten to dissolve: prosaically substantial though these scenes of suburban life appear throughout most of the action, as Humphrey drives past the Rye

he saw the children playing there and the women coming home from work with their shopping-bags, the Rye for an instant looking like a cloud of green and gold, the people seeming to ride upon it, as you might say there was another world than this.

This kind of last-sentence taking-off from the material and circumscribed world of the novel's action has, even this early in Muriel Spark's career, become standard practice, and the transfiguration of the commonplace world, as in one of Blake's mystical lyrics, seems to have behind it the passage from Traherne which had been drawn on for one of the epigraphs of *Memento Mori*. What has seemed a light-hearted comic fantasy abruptly deepens into an utterance of transcendental joy.

On the penultimate page of the novel, in the paragraph that, parodying the traditional winding-up chapter, tells the reader of 'Dougal's subsequent life', we learn that eventually 'for economy's sake, he gathered together the scrap ends of his profligate experience – for he was a frugal man at heart – and turned them into a lot of cock-eyed books, and went far in the world'. Dougal, it seems, is not only a fictional maker of fictions and a close relative of the Father of Lies but an author and perhaps even *the* author, as Caroline Rose is both protagonist and, ultimately, 'author' of *The Comforters*. It takes an emissary, even a diabolic emissary, from 'another world than this' to shake us out of our complacencies and compel our recognition of that world's existence. Making a joke partly directed at herself, the author seems to be suggesting that the novelist does the Devil's work for him and that the Devil can also be a novelist. To this extent the *Ballad* can be seen as complementary to *The Comforters*, where the 'novel' seemed at times to be authored by God, and also as having something in common with *Memento Mori*, where another visitant from 'another world', Death himself, was invoked to show us that the mundane world with its 'shopping-bags' and other material preoccupations is not all there is.

The title of *The Bachelors* seems to promise a novel of 'character', social observation and ironic comedy. It is indeed that, but not only that. There is an abundance of characters in this short novel, which is also heavily plotted; but as usual with Muriel Spark these are means and not ends. The opening, with its emphasis on time and place, seems to assert a vein of realism:

> Daylight was appearing over London, the great city of bachelors. Half-pint bottles of milk began to be stood on the doorsteps of houses containing single apartments from Hampstead Heath to Greenwich Park, and from Wanstead

Flats to Putney Heath; but especially in Hampstead, especially
in Kensington.

We soon learn that it is a Saturday morning, and the action
extends over only four days, to the following Tuesday. It is, we
can deduce, late September: Patrick Seton tells Elsie that his
non-existent divorce suit 'comes up' on 25 November, '"In a
couple of months"' (p. 23: this and subsequent references are to
the Penguin edition), and Matthew Finch says that it is his
birthday and that he comes '"under the sign of Libra"', the
zodiacal period beginning on 23 September (p. 67).
There is a good deal of this kind of particularity about days
and times (Patrick's appointment with Dr Lyte, for instance, is
at 'half-past twelve sharp'), but the time scheme has some odd
features. A few pages after he has declared that it is his birthday,
Matthew tells Patrick '"My birthday was last week"' (p. 75),
making the remark 'aimlessly as a boy-seminar answering a tall
black frock'. Both the statement and the narrator's comment are
puzzling: it appears to be a pointless lie told automatically, as
by one answering the questions of a catechist. More radically
puzzling is a kind of slippage in the chronological narrative.
Many chapters and episodes contain at or near their beginning
some reference to the day or the time of day or both: thus at the
beginning of Chapter 2 it is still Saturday, and later in the same
chapter it is 'Saturday night' (p. 34); when Chapter 3 opens it
is Sunday, and it is still Sunday when Elsie calls on Matthew
(p. 50); at the beginning of Chapter 4 Patrick reflects that he
must appear at the Magistrate's Court at ten in the morning of
the next day, and since it has already been stated (p. 22) that
his case will come up on Tuesday, this must be Monday. But at
the beginning of Chapter 10 it is Sunday again, and at the end
of the same long chapter it is the early hours of Monday morning
(p. 167). Novelists since Conrad have made use of the 'time-
shift', which holds no mysteries for students of the modern novel;
but the apparently innocent and guileless narrative art of Muriel
Spark up to this point in her development hardly prepares us
for such devices, and it may be that she is gently mocking the
preoccupation of the novel with time in the same way that
Samuel Beckett, in such novels as *Murphy* and *Watt*, mocks
the novel's preoccupation with circumstantiality and logic by
creating impossible situations within banal settings (on the first

page of *Murphy*, a hero who has tied himself hand and foot into a rocking-chair).

The narrowness of the time scheme, like the restricting of the locale to a few districts of London, confers on *The Bachelors* a concentration that is heightened by another device that Muriel Spark may have borrowed from the early novels of Evelyn Waugh: the construction of a section of the novel by juxtaposing short episodes, involving different groups of characters, that may all be supposed to be taking place at about the same time. In Chapter 11, for example, successive sections begin 'Tim Raymond sat . . .', 'Ewart Thornton sat . . .', 'Marlene sat . . .', 'Walter Prett leaned . . .', 'Elsie telephoned . . .', and the stylistic parallels convey a sense of simultaneity, of observing with a god-like eye the working out of many different lives held together by their common existence in a great city.

The Bachelors imitates *Memento Mori* in having a complex plot that has the air of parody of the plotting in a traditional novel: perjury, blackmail (a crime in the past threatened with disclosure), forgery and a stolen letter are devices that recall the Victorian 'sensation novel'; and like many Victorian novels *The Bachelors* moves towards its climax in a trial scene. In the same way, some of the characters – the unscrupulous pseudo-priest Father Socket, for example, or Dr Mike Garland, clairvoyant, homosexual and petty criminal – seem, even in their Dickensian or Waugh-like names, to draw attention to their own fictionality. As usual with Muriel Spark, however, discussions of plot and character rarely take one to the heart of the novel, the real interest of which lies in its unobtrusively hinted themes and ideas.

In all the lengthy character list two men emerge as having more than individual and local interest, and moreover as having a suggestive if problematic relationship to each other: Patrick Seton, spiritualistic medium and confidence trickster, and Ronald Bridges, graphologist and epileptic. Socially and morally they occupy different worlds, but there are hidden links between them. When Patrick blackmails Dr Lyte into giving him a supply of a new drug, it is described as one that has been 'employed for experimental purposes, to induce epileptic convulsions in rats, and which, taken in certain minor quantities, greatly improved both the spectacular quality of Patrick's trances and his actual psychic powers' (p. 61). Later, at Patrick's trial,

Ronald is called as an expert witness and suffers an epileptic seizure under the stress of giving evidence:

> Ronald swayed. He fumbled in his pockets for his pills. They were in his other suit, at home. He gave up. He stumbled down the steps and fell two steps before he got to the bottom. There he foamed at the mouth. His eyes turned upwards, and the drum-like kicking of his heels began on the polished wooden floor.
> 'Is this man a medium?' said the judge. (p. 198)

The judge's question is a reasonable one, for he has earlier listened to a description of Patrick's behaviour during one of his mediumistic trances: '"Let us get this clear," said the judge. 'A person in a state of trance as you call it, rolls up his or her eyes, foams at the mouth, and twitches . . ."' (p. 195).

A connection is thus made between these two very different men, and between the one's fraudulent make-believe and the other's genuine and life-long affliction. Patrick seeks to impose on credulous clients by claiming to put them in touch with a world of spirits occupying a remarkably materialistic Heaven in which the petty preoccupations of life on earth persist; Ronald, a Catholic, seems to use his affliction to move towards a state of grace: at the end of Chapter 8, he has a severe epileptic attack and we are told that 'This often happened to Ronald after he had made some effort of will towards graciousness, as if a devil in his body was taking its revenge' (p. 112). He resembles the man possessed with a devil, driven out by Jesus Christ, as recounted in the Gospels, and Patrick, whose surname is so close to 'Satan', is his opposite (like Hogg's 'justified sinner' he is convinced of his own superiority to considerations of right and wrong, good and evil, as he plots to murder the girl he has promised to marry). Put in these terms, *The Bachelors* is less a social comedy or a tale of crime outwitted than an allegory of the struggle between the forces of light and darkness.

There is also an obvious contrast between Patrick's claims to put people in touch with a spiritual world and Ronald's unpretentious and uncommercialised wisdom and understanding:

> 'What do you think,' Martin said, 'goes on in a man like

Patrick Seton's mind when he looks back on his life?'

People frequently asked this sort of question of Ronald. It was as if they held some ancient superstition about his epilepsy: 'the falling sickness', 'the sacred disease', 'the evil spirit'. Ronald felt he was regarded by his friends as a sacred cow or a wise monkey. He was, perhaps, touchy on the point. Sometimes, he thought, after all, they would have come to him with their deep troubles, consulted him on the nature of things, listened to his wise old words, even if he wasn't an afflicted man. If he had been a priest, people would have consulted him in the same way. (p. 64)

Ronald has been disappointed in his vocation, having been rejected for the priesthood, but the implication here is that as an epileptic he is a kind of secular priest and the passage echoes a conversation much earlier in the book:

> . . . it was an old priest speaking – 'you were never meant to be a first-rate careerist.'
> 'Only a first-rate epileptic?'
> 'Indeed, yes. Quite seriously, yes,' the old priest said. . . . (p. 12)

If Ronald's surname may also be taken symbolically, his role seems to be that of a genuine 'bridge' or medium (unlike the other kind of 'medium', with its pretensions to fake spirituality, that Patrick claims to be) between the material and the immaterial world.

Ronald is conscious of the special status accorded him by an affliction that is both a contemporary medical problem treated with modern drugs and an ancient phenomenon known by a variety of names and surrounded by superstition. When a girl reproaches him with being snobbish ('"You think I'm not good enough for you. . . . Not your class"') he replies: '"I'm an epileptic. . . . It rather puts one out of the reach of class"' (p. 167). It also puts him, by his own judgement, out of the reach of marriage, and this has the curious effect of linking him with Patrick, for whom marriage has no place in the scheme of things, and setting him apart from most of the other characters (as he says, '"Everyone consults me about their marriages"' (p. 75) – again, the priest-like role). The resemblance between the two men is, however, more apparent than real, for while Patrick has the 'enlightened' views on marriage of an old-fashioned freethinker ('"I've always believed in free love. I've never believed in marriage," Patrick murmured. . . . Fergusson tilted back his chair and heard him out: man-made laws, suppression of the individual, relics of the Victorian era . . .': p. 91), Ronald's conviction that his disability sets him apart and rules out choices available to others is closer to that of St Paul, another sufferer from a 'thorn in the flesh' and one who conceded only that it is 'better to marry than to burn'.[36]

What has been said about the profoundly antithetical presentation of the two main characters makes it difficult to accept Alan Bold's reading of the novel. For him it is 'an exposure of the emptiness of spurious religions', and he includes Ronald, who 'has missed his priestly vocation', on his list of those who are 'all, in various degrees, frauds'.[37] But Ronald is surely an exception to what Bold calls the 'moral vacuity' of the characters in this novel: he stands for a sincere, if only partially successful, attempt to attain wisdom and grace, and there is surely a symbolic significance in his profession, for a graphologist is one who seeks to interpret correctly signs that may be meaningless or mysterious to others, and Ronald's speciality lies in distinguishing between authentic and fraudulent documents – in other words, in pursuing the truth.

Much more cogent and persuasive, to my mind, is the reading offered by Peter Kemp, who takes as his starting point a passage in Muriel Spark's essay on Proust in which she draws attention to the 'dualistic attitude towards matter and spirit' in contemporary Christian creative writing. Kemp sees *The Comforters* as embodying 'a philosophy which combats dualism and, as it were, salvages the everyday by seeing it as permeated by the spiritual': as Muriel Spark said in an interview published in the *Sunday Times* in 1962, 'I think we're all involved in the supernatural world'. Kemp views Ronald Bridges as 'the writer's persona in the novel' (a 'bridge' between novelist and reader?) and observes that 'there are strong similarities implied between Ronald's situation and that of the novelist'. Romantic artists (not that Muriel Spark is quite that) are prone to talk of their 'demon', and an epileptic seizure has something superficially in common with the state of possession exhibited by a prophet or oracle: 'As the book proceeds, the suggestion is elaborated that Ronald's disability, his wound, entails some compensatory penetration, has endowed him with more than ordinary perception; and that, in its turn, this gift can be uncomfortable, generating acrid states of mind . . .'.[38] If Ronald had written a novel, we might say, it would not have been very unlike one of Muriel Spark's. Seton's spiritualism, on the other hand, is a corrupt or debased quasi-religion that insists on the dualism of the material and the spiritual worlds with its claims for 'the after-life' and 'the spirit world'. As Matthew Finch says of Patrick Seton, ' "The man's a dualist. No sacramental sense" ' (p. 84), and a few lines later Matthew declares, ' "It shows a dualistic attitude, not to marry if you aren't going to be a priest or a religious. You've got to affirm the oneness of reality in one form or another" ' (p. 85).

As one who has a priestly vocation, and fulfils a kind of priestly function as counsellor to his friends, Ronald is the exception that proves the rule, but no such claim can be made for Patrick, whose self-sufficiency is a kind of egotism or hubris that rejects God as well as society and its laws and his fellow beings. And so we return to the point at which we started, the novel's title; and it is by now clear that bachelorhood is not just a social phenomenon or a means of stimulating plot interest, but a symbol of failure to achieve 'the oneness of reality'. As Kemp argues, the novel places much emphasis on 'the sterile and the unproductive: upon homosexuality, contraception, and abortion, all of which are treated with distaste'. Other characters aspire towards marriage, but outside both groups stands Ronald, who thinks of himself 'as one possessed by a demon' and who is 'at certain tense moments, a truth-machine, under which his friends took on the aspect of demon-hypocrites' (p. 14). This makes him one of Muriel Spark's select band of truth-tellers, like Caroline Rose in *The Comforters* and Jean Taylor in *Memento Mori*, just as Patrick Seton is a more sinister version of Dougal Douglas in *The Ballad of Peckham Rye*.

More sinister: and this is, as Ruth Whittaker has emphasised, a darker novel than its predecessors. 'The murky atmosphere of *The Bachelors* is of deception, emotional and moral expediency, of people battening on one another with leech-like singlemindedness'.[39] The two novels that follow it are shorter and noticeably more light-hearted – or such, at least, is the immediate impression they make, though it is always as well to reserve judgement with a writer who often seems to arouse the expectation of one kind of story before giving us an entirely different kind.

The Prime of Miss Jean Brodie was a considerable popular and commercial success and was adapted for the stage and the screen. Such transformations can seriously distort the meaning of the original text, and (for instance) Maggie Smith's bravura performance as Jean Brodie, richly entertaining though it is, conveys a misleading impression of the character in the novel. Francis Russell Hart has stated forcefully the real nature of the novel's protagonist:

> Jean Brodie is one of the spiritual tyrants, whose egoistic romanticism is the link between an obsessive Calvinist doctrine of the Elect, of Justification, and the fascism of Mussolini and Franco. . . .[40]

One of the critical problems raised by this novel is that of reconciling the darkness of this central purpose with the apparent lightness of the surface.

This lightness derives partly from an element of parody, partly from a distancing of the world of the novel in place and time. Earlier novels had parodied the detective story and the island story; now Muriel Spark turns to the school story with its traditional cloistered and timeless world of innocence. Many of the ingredients of this novel – the old-fashioned girls' school for the daughters of the Edinburgh bourgeoisie, the suspicious headmistress, the one-armed art master, the middle-aged spinster schoolmistress – seem to belong to farce or comedy of manners, but these promises of undisturbing entertainment are not fulfilled and the story shades into a theological drama with tragic overtones. Jean Brodie is guilty of the sin of presumption: her motive in appropriating a group of girls as 'the Brodie set' is not a quasi-maternal or pedagogical concern for their welfare or their intellectual development (though it sometimes looks like that) but a craving to usurp the role of God (which is also the role of the novelist) by determining the future lives of 'her' girls. What she calls the 'crème de la crème' are, in Calvinistic terms, the Elect. Her boast, ' "Give me a girl at an impressionable age, and she is mine for life" ' (Penguin edition, p. 9) not only reveals her possessiveness but recalls the Jesuit claim that influences in the formative years are never shaken off (' "Would that I had been given charge of you girls when you were seven. I sometimes fear it's too late, now . . ."', she later remarks: p. 22). In her bid to secure for ever a girl's mind and soul, Miss Brodie recalls, once again, the Satanic figure in James Hogg's novel. The delightfully attractive and independent-minded heroine of dramatic versions of Muriel Spark's book is revealed by a careful reading of the text as egotistical, menacing and even satanic.

It is true, however, that the setting of the story, Edinburgh in the Thirties, tends to encourage the view of *The Prime of Miss Jean Brodie* as a comic tale of an engagingly dotty heroine in a quaint 'period' setting. Turning aside from the postwar London settings favoured in most of her preceding novels, Muriel Spark sets the main action in Edinburgh, the city of her own birth, in the 1930s, the period of her own adolescence: twelve years old when the decade began, she could have been a member of Miss Brodie's set. References to events and personalities of the period – Hitler's rise to power in 1933, the Silver Jubilee of George V in 1935, the Spanish Civil War breaking out in 1936, popular film stars such as Norma Shearer and Elizabeth Bergner – place the small world of middle-class Edinburgh in the context of European events, with Miss Brodie's summer holidays in Italy and Germany, duly reported on to her girls, acting as an unreliable link between the two.

Since this is a story of long-term effects, however, it cannot be confined to a single decade, and many of the numerous time references antedate or postdate the Thirties. Miss Brodie was born in or about 1890, if we are to believe her story (p. 12) of an engagement in 1914 to a young man killed in 1918 at the age of 22 and six years younger than herself. This birthdate has a certain appropriateness as the beginning of the decade that saw the climax of the Aesthetic Movement: Miss Brodie's favourite poets include Keats and Tennyson, the forerunners of that movement; she also quotes Walter Pater and proffers the Mona Lisa, with her enviable 'composure', as a model of deportment. She dies, 'just after' the Second World War, at the age of fifty-five (pp. 27, 56), after being forced into premature retirement. But the timescale of the novel extends beyond this and almost up to the date of composition, for the allusions to the subsequent life of Miss Brodie's girls include a visit by Monica to 'Sandy at the nunnery in the late nineteen-fifties' (p. 55). One sees why the main action has to be set in the previous generation: it is

only thus that the far-reaching effects of the Brodie influence can
be traced.

It is, then, a novel precisely located in time and one in which
the events of private lives are related both to contemporary
public history and to the subsequent fortunes of those lives.
But the narrative method is far from being straightforwardly
chronological: frequent time-shifts, and especially flashforwards,
bring together happenings widely separated in time, and, as in
a modernist novel such as Conrad's *The Secret Agent* or Ford
Madox Ford's *The Good Soldier*, the effects of suspense and
uncertainty are partly sacrificed in the interests of a dramatic
juxtaposition that compels the reader to relate causes to their
distant effects. A paragraph that begins 'This was the first winter
of the two years that this class spent with Miss Brodie. It had
turned nineteen-thirty-one . . .' goes on to refer to Eunice
Gardiner as one of the favoured girls and then continues: 'It was
twenty-eight years after Eunice did the splits in Miss Brodie's
flat . . .' (i.e., 1960; the novel appeared in 1961), and with the
recounting of Eunice's wish to visit Miss Brodie's grave (pp. 25–
7). The action of the novel is not open-ended: as in a Greek
tragedy, it moves towards a conclusion known well in advance.
Similarly, schoolgirl speculations about their teachers are revived
a generation later as the narrative turns without warning from
the early Thirties to the late Fifties:

> 'Rose is the only one who believes me,' said Monica Douglas.
> When she visited Sandy at the nunnery in the late nineteen-
> fifties, Monica said, 'I really did see Teddy Lloyd kiss Miss
> Brodie in the art room one day.'
> 'I know you did,' said Sandy. (p. 55).

And on the next page Miss Brodie's reference to her 'prime'
prompts a switch to a future hidden from her but not from the
narrator, whose stance is in the reader's present:

> She had reckoned on her prime lasting till she was sixty.
> But this, the year after the war, was in fact Miss Brodie's last
> and fifty-sixth year. (p. 56)

A degree of chronological agility is therefore called for from
the reader of this narrative. Within three lines (p. 10) the action

can move back six years, from 1936 to 1930; shortly afterwards
it goes back to 1914 (p. 12), forward to 1943 (p. 14), back again
by stages to 1940 (p. 15) and the beginning of the Thirties
(p. 25). The current events of the main action are, for the reader,
part of history. It is thus a novel in which we are constantly
required to see human words and actions, if not quite in the
light of eternity, at least in relation to the future. This is especially
true of the issue that forms both the main plot interest of the
novel and its moral centre: the betrayal of Miss Brodie by one
of her own girls. The headmistress's plot to rid her staff of the
progressive and unpliable Jean Brodie provokes the questions:
will she succeed? and if so, how? Miss Brodie's tragedy is that
she is betrayed by one of her own girls, as Christ was by one of
the Twelve. Judas Iscariot was traditionally depicted with red
hair, and Miss Brodie is betrayed by Sandy.
  One of Muriel Spark's critics has argued that

> it is Sandy who is the true centre of the novel. However
> peripherally or obliquely it is presented, her conversion . . . is
> at the novel's core. Of all the members of the Brodie set, it is
> Sandy who feels Miss Brodie's influence most keenly, most
> deeply. She is the most like her, the one credited with 'insight',
> the one who acts as her proxy in the love affair with Teddy
> Lloyd (even though Miss Brodie has originally cast Rose
> Stanley for the part), the one who betrays her.[41]

'Betray' and 'betrayal' are keywords of the novel. Confident of
her ability to outwit the headmistress's machinations, Miss
Brodie tells her girls '"I do not think ever to be betrayed"'
(p. 39), but later, 'shrivelled and betrayed' (p. 56), she
expresses – ironically enough, to Sandy, whom she does not
suspect – her puzzlement:

> '. . . nobody could prove what was between Gordon Lowther
> and myself. It was never proved. It was not on those grounds
> that I was betrayed. I should like to know who betrayed me.
> It is incredible that it should have been one of my own girls.
> I often wonder if it was poor Mary. . . .' (p. 60)

Only at the end of her life, learning of Sandy's conversion, does
she suspect the truth. Her reaction to discovering that Sandy

has entered a convent characteristically arouses irritation at this
evidence of the failure of her own early influence:

> 'What a waste. That is not the sort of dedication I meant.
> Do you think she has done this to annoy me? I begin to wonder
> if it was not Sandy who betrayed me.' (p. 63)

This falls with startling effect, cutting as it does into a passage
set a generation earlier in which Miss Brodie is commending to
Sandy the 'dedication' of the ballet dancer Anna Pavlova. In
retiring from the world, the adult Sandy has taken all too
seriously Miss Brodie's lesson of dedication.

Allan Massie's claim that Sandy is the 'true centre of the
novel' may be overstated, but there is no doubt at all that she is
the one who really understands Miss Brodie, with a clear-eyed,
dispassionate vision of the hidden and even the unconscious
springs of her actions. It is Sandy who realises that she is both
greedy for power over the girls' lives and prepared to use them
to act out her own desires and fantasies: 'Sandy looked at her,
and perceived that the woman was obsessed by the need for
Rose to sleep with the man she herself was in love with' (p. 119).
Illustrating A. S. Byatt's general observation that there are in
Muriel Spark's work 'many characters with *alter egos* – doubles,
ghosts, self-projections, split personalities caused by a mixed
racial heritage or religious conflict',[42] Miss Brodie, part Calvinist,
part Romantic, defines her own relationship to the man into
whose carnal embraces she is prepared to thrust one of the girls
in her care:

> 'I am his Muse,' said Miss Brodie. 'But I have renounced
> his love in order to dedicate my prime to the young girls in
> my care. I am his Muse but Rose shall take my place.'
> She thinks she is Providence, thought Sandy, she thinks she
> is the God of Calvin, she sees the beginning and the end.
> (p. 120)

But only God and the novelist can see the beginning and the
end, and Miss Brodie's plans misfire: the girl who has at her
urging gone to fight in Spain is killed in a train crash; the
dictators whom she has enthusiastically greeted as heroes (in
1933 Hitler is for her 'a prophet-figure like Thomas Carlyle':

p. 97) turn out to be tyrants and mass-murderers; and Sandy betrays her. Jean Brodie is not merely misguided and irresponsible: her attempts to play Providence are wicked. She is Calvinistic in her conviction of her own rightness and superiority to others, and (as Sandy says near the end) '"a born Fascist"' (p. 125) in her wish to dominate and mould the lives of others.

The final image of the novel, and its final words, belong to Sandy, who has achieved fame through her 'strange book of psychology' titled 'The Transfiguration of the Commonplace' (not a bad motto for Muriel Spark's fiction), but who is immured in her convent, 'clutching the bars of her grille more desperately than ever' (p. 128). She has betrayed Miss Brodie but in the last words of the novel is driven to confess the dead woman's permanent and inescapable influence as she replies to an interviewer's question:

> 'What were the main influences of your school days, Sister Helena? Were they literary or political or personal? Was it Calvinism?'
> Sandy said: 'There was a Miss Jean Brodie in her prime.'

The last of the novels of what is here designated as her early period, *The Girls of Slender Means*, shows Muriel Spark moving even further in the direction that is to characterise much of her later work, towards the sparely written, impersonally narrated, fable-like form that she has made her own. Like its immediate predecessor it has a lightness of surface that is belied by its fundamental seriousness, and leads towards a crucial and unexpected conversion. It also resembles *The Prime of Miss Jean Brodie* in its mainly female character list and in its setting of the main action in a period within living memory but belonging unmistakably to the past.

The opening words of this novel of 1963 are the same as the closing words: 'Long ago in 1945' – a phrase that seems to blend the precision of history with the romantic vagueness of fairy tale, folktale or fable. There are numerous allusions to contemporary events: VE Day (the end of the war in Europe, on 8 May 1945), VJ night (the end of war with Japan, whose surrender was made on 14 August 1945), the A Bomb (the US dropped an atom bomb on Hiroshima on 6 August 1945), the General Election (the Labour Party won a landslide victory on 26 July 1945), as well as popular songs and personalities of the period. The setting is a London full of bomb sites: the phrase 'stony rubble' in the opening paragraph is perhaps a deliberate echo of 'stony rubbish' in the most famous of postwar poems, T. S. Eliot's *The Waste Land* of 1922; and most of the action takes place in or near a women's hostel, the May of Teck Club, situated 'obliquely opposite the site of the Memorial' – that is, the Albert Memorial in Kensington. Muriel Spark is back on familiar ground, the locale of *The Comforters* and *The Bachelors* as well as of novels still unwritten. The May of Teck Club has not survived the bombing of London unscathed, having been 'three times window-shattered since 1940' (the first of a number of references to the number three, probably significant in view of the author's later, more fully explicit interest in numerology). There is also, as it turns out, an unexploded bomb in the garden.

Most of the characters are girls, or older women, living in the hostel, and one of the meanings to be attached to their 'slender means' is the nun-like poverty in which they live in this period of rationing and official 'austerity'. Again the point is made in the opening sentence and repeated in the novel's closing words: 'Long ago in 1945 all the nice people in England were poor . . .'; '. . . the May of Teck establishment in its meek, unselfconscious attitudes of poverty long ago in 1945'. The residents include Joanna Childe, a rector's daughter who is a lover of poetry and is training to be a teacher of elocution; Selina Redwood, a beauty much preoccupied with her own elegance and poise; Jane Wright, a fat and unattractive girl who works for a publisher and makes considerable social capital out of her claims that she is engaged in 'brainwork'; Pauline Fox, a mentally unbalanced girl who has fantasies of going out to dinner with the popular musical comedy star of the period, Jack Buchanan; and several others. The older generation of residents is represented by three spinsters, Greggie, Collie and Jarvie. One of the few male characters is Nicholas Farringdon, a frequent visitor to the Club, of whom one of the girls says at the end of the story, '"I think he was in love with us all, poor fellow"'.

As in *The Prime of Miss Jean Brodie*, the story is one of great simplicity: by this stage Muriel Spark is leaving behind the complex plots found in some of her earlier novels. And as in its immediate predecessor, *The Girls of Slender Means* from time to time fractures the steady progress of a narrative that frequently

draws attention to dates and public events, and allows us a
glimpse, as through a crack in the fabric of time, of what the
future holds. Thus, in Chapter 4:

> Meantime, Nicholas touched lightly on the imagination of
> the girls of slender means, and they on his. He had not yet
> slept on the roof with Selina on the hot summer nights – he
> gaining access from the American-occupied attic of the hotel
> next door, and she through the slit window – and he had not
> yet witnessed that action of savagery so extreme that it forced
> him involuntarily to make an entirely unaccustomed gesture,
> the signing of the cross upon himself. At this time Nicholas
> still worked for one of those left-handed departments of the
> Foreign Office, the doings of which the right hand did not
> know.

The rhetorical structure of this passage, in which the keywords
are 'Meantime . . . not yet . . . not yet . . . At this time . . .',
indicates the brief intrusion of the future upon events that belong
to an unfolding present. A few lines later comes another glimpse
of the future, as one of the girls tells another in a telephone
conversation that ' "Nick Farringdon's dead" '; then, within a
few more lines, the living Nick comes 'to dine at the club' and
is intoxicated by 'the beautiful aspects of poverty and charm
amongst these girls in the brown-papered drawing room'. These
reminders of what the future holds in store for some of the
characters endows their trivial acts with a kind of solemnity: the
commonplace Nicholas takes on a profound seriousness when
we learn that, after a revelation that leads to his conversion, he
will become a monk and suffer a martyr's death in Haiti, just as
Sandy the schoolgirl in the earlier novel is redeemed from
banality by the juxtaposed image of the older Sandy, a nun
clutching the grille that excludes her from the world.
  Similarly, the bomb in the garden that explodes near the end
of the book has been 'promised' from an early stage. The effect
of the bomb is to reduce the structure to a state of imminent
collapse, and the outcome is a rescue and a death. The rescue,
by Selina, is not of a human being but of a Schiaparelli dress,
and it is this apparently trivial act that fills Nicholas with horror,
and leads to his instinctively making the sign of the cross, to his
conversion, and ultimately to his martyrdom. For, as a

manuscript note left by him after his death and quoted very near the end of the book puts it, 'a vision of evil may be as effective to conversion as a vision of good'.

For some critics Selina's action and Nicholas's reaction constitute too frail a centre of gravity for the book to be effective. Patricia Stubbs, for instance, suggests that

> the central event, which could be regarded as [the novel's] climax, is slight. . . . The mind is meant to rest on this novel in a delighted and amused fashion, not subjecting its meaning and structure to the enquiries of logic and reason, since it is not framed to answer their demands.[43]

This seems a serious misreading and missing of the point. There wasn't after all much 'logic and reason' about Paul's vision on the road to Damascus, and as for describing as slight a climax which involves a death and indirectly leads to another death, one might object that the parables of Jesus are slight enough. The refrain from a popular song of the period recurs frequently in the text:

> There were angels dining at the Ritz,
> And a nightingale sang in Berkeley Square. . . .

and the slick modish words have a relevance to the serious business of the novel, for here, as often elsewhere, Muriel Spark is urging that there are angels and devils in everyday life.[44] The notion has received comic treatment in *The Ballad of Peckham Rye*, but here it is entirely serious.

Even in terms of realistic psychological motivation, however, the climactic scene is convincing. Nicholas has been presented as an idealist: 'his austere bed-sitting room' has a monkish quality, and he sleeps with Selina 'with the aim of converting her soul' as well as willing 'the awakening of her social conscience':

> With the reckless ambition of a visionary, he pushed his passion for Selina into a desire that she, too, should accept and exploit the outlines of poverty in her life. He loved her as he loved his native country. He wanted Selina to be an ideal society personified amongst her bones, he wanted her beautiful limbs to obey her mind and heart like intelligent men and

women, and for these to possess the same grace and beauty
as her body. Whereas Selina's desires were comparatively
humble, she only wanted, at that particular moment, a packet
of hair-grips which had just then disappeared from the shops
for a few weeks. (Chapter 7)

As the last sentence indicates, with its abrupt descent from the
visionary to the banal, Selina is unworthy of his idealising love:
a thoroughgoing materialist, she is more interested in his clothing
coupons than his ideals, and her carefully cultivated and much
envied 'poise' is actually a kind of solipsism, a callous indifference
to the needs and even the very existence of others. She thus has
something in common with an earlier quasi-diabolical figure,
Patrick Seton in *The Bachelors*.

The explosion of the bomb causes not only the literal destruction of the house but the metaphorical destruction of Nicholas's
idealised vision of Selina: his sudden apprehension of her supreme
selfishness in returning to the house for the dress when others
are in danger of their lives is an Aristotelian moment of
'discovery'. 'Is it safe?' she asks him as she emerges – meaning,
of course, 'safe for *me*'; his reply, 'Nowhere's safe', is theological
rather than mundane in its application – nowhere in the world
are we safe from wickedness, from the evil from which we pray
to be delivered. The reader is already aware that Nicholas's
notion of the May of Teck Club as a kind of Eden or Utopia
bears only a limited relation to the truth: there is pettiness, envy,
selfishness and even madness within its walls, so that it is no
bad emblem or microcosm of the world itself. Selina's rescue of
the Schiaparelli evening dress may be a 'slight' incident, but in
human life great issues can hang upon seemingly trivial events,
and Nicholas's reaction to this 'epiphany' is momentous. The
incident resolves, if any resolution is needed, the ambiguity
inherent in Selina's name (worth speculating on because Muriel
Spark is habitually sensitive to the implications of namings);
'Selina' may be derived through the French 'Céline' from the
Latin *caelum* (heaven), but another derivation (perhaps in fact a
false etymology) turns out to be the relevant one – from the
Greek for 'moon', a heavenly body of great beauty but cold,
remote and indifferent.

Joanna Childe, on the other hand, is mentally compared by
Nicholas at one point to the Virgin Mary, and it may be

significant that she shares the initials of Jesus Christ. It is not only her clerical background, her love of poetry, and her death in the collapsing building that mark her as Selina's opposite: she is also one of Muriel Spark's truthtellers, like Jean Taylor in *Memento Mori* and Ronald Bridges in *The Bachelors*, and the poems she recites usually have a relevance, or even a prophetic quality, that endows her with the role of a commentator or chorus. As an elocutionist, constantly practising her art within the walls of the hostel and heard by its residents, she is one of Muriel Spark's 'voices': in this case a human agent transmitting a message with spiritual significance. She recites the closing lines of Coleridge's 'Kubla Khan', and these seem to have a bearing on Nicholas's subsequent fate:

> For he on honey-dew hath fed,
> And drunk the milk of Paradise.

Lines from Coleridge's 'Ancient Mariner' describing the Devil have a relevance to Selina's later diabolical act. And the fate of the nun in Hopkins's 'Wreck of the Deutschland' prefigures her own fate in another kind of disaster, while her recitation of Wordsworth's lines on Chatterton also seem to relate to her own early death. Nor is it inappropriate that a reference to Nicholas's idealised attachment to the May of Teck Club in general and Selina in particular should be immediately followed by some lines by Byron expressive of a romantic dream. In this close-knit, tightly written book nothing is wasted or superfluous, nothing there simply for local effect: collectively, Joanna's recitations add up to a kind of alternative narrative, or at least a highlighting of the crucial issues of the main narrative.

'The transfiguration of the commonplace', the subject and title of Sandy's book in *The Prime of Miss Jean Brodie*, is an apt summary of *The Girls of Slender Means* and indeed of an important element in the best of Muriel Spark's fiction. Under the intense light shed by this short, scrupulously thrifty narrative, the banal lives of a rather ordinary group of characters at a period of history when life in England was drab and comfortless take on a kind of radiance that, once again, may remind us of the passage from Traherne's *Centuries of Meditation* drawn on in one of the epigraphs to *Memento Mori*.

I have spoken of the narrative as thrifty, but right at the end occurs an incident that seems gratuitous, even pointless: in the huge crowd outside Buckingham Palace on VJ night, a seaman 'observed only by Nicholas, slid a knife silently between the ribs of a woman who was with him'. These anonymous figures, and the unexplained violence, have the quality of allegory, even though the setting is historically authentic. That Nicholas is the witness of this apparently meaningless and presumably unpunished crime may offer an explanation: Selina's conduct on the roof (a place where they had formerly made love) has made him aware of evil in the world, and now – ironically, among the jubilant crowds – that awareness receives confirmation. It is also, of course, part of an evil that is global in scale, for the event occurs only a few days after the dropping of the bomb on Hiroshima: this is, implicitly, a novel about *two* bombs being exploded, one in the microcosm of the May of Teck Club, and in a work of fiction, the other in a distant land and in the newspapers and history books. Puzzling though the knifing episode may be on a first reading, it takes its place in the pattern of a novel whose apparent simplicity, like its apparent lightness of tone, is deceptive: nothing could be more serious than Nicholas's vision of evil, and even after several rereadings it is a book that has the power to puzzle and challenge. Any criticism that attempts to 'explain' this author's meaning by paraphrase of her ideas risks misrepresentation, for these are novels that at their best have the quality of a modern poem, subtle, allusive, not the less rewarding for being less than fully explicable.

By 1963, then, after less than seven years as a published novelist, Muriel Spark had notched up the remarkable tally of seven novels. She had moreover come to be recognised as a talent and a voice of a highly distinctive kind: as one who had made it clear both what she was interested in doing and what she was not willing to do, and as one who had implicitly defined her own position in relation to the British tradition of fiction as still practised by most of her contemporaries.

In one of Muriel Spark's early short stories, 'Come Along, Marjorie', collected in *The Go-Away Bird* (1958), the heroine-narrator, who has much in common with the heroines of the early novels, is spending some time at Watling Abbey, a Catholic retreat built 'on the site of an ancient Temple of Mithras' and mainly patronised by those 'recovering from nerves'. At one point the heroine is awaiting a telephone call from the outside world ('from Jonathan, my very best friend') and is approached in the cloisters by Miss Pettigrew, a strange woman who never speaks:

> I was so bemused by my need to talk to Jonathan that I thought, as she approached, 'Perhaps they've sent her to call me.' Immediately I remembered, that was absurd, for she carried no messages ever. But she continued so directly towards me that I thought again, 'She's going to speak.' She had her dark eyes on my face. . . .
> 'Excuse me,' she said, 'I have a message for you.'
> I was so relieved that I forgot to be surprised by her speaking.
> 'Am I wanted on the telephone?' I said, half-ready to run across to the office.
> 'No, I have a message for you,' she said.
> 'What's the message?'
> 'The Lord is risen,' she said.

The tiny exchange prefigures a major element in Muriel Spark's fiction: this unlikely angelic messenger summons the heroine back from her worldly preoccupations to thoughts of higher things, and while, given the somewhat bizarre setting, there is nothing non-realistic in what happens, there is a strong sense of the supernatural impinging upon and transforming the mundane. This is what may be called the 'Angels at the Ritz' motif, the use of a human or non-human messenger to issue a reminder that, for all our material preoccupations, we live in a world that not only has a spiritual dimension but whose materialism is transfigured by the transcendental.

That this should be shown dramatically, through epiphanies or moments of peculiar insight, almost inevitably has implications for the kind of fiction that emerges and its relationship to traditions of realism. There is a partial severing of the realist 'contract' in the early novels – in the mysterious voices and typewriter, and the witch-like Mrs Hogg, in *The Comforters*, the telephone calls in *Memento Mori*, the diabolical figure in *The Ballad of Peckham Rye* – though it is noteworthy that in the last three novels discussed in this chapter this element becomes less overt or even disappears entirely: the devil-figure of *The Bachelors*

does not have even vestigial horns on his head, the moment of
pure evil seen by Nicholas in *The Girls of Slender Means* is
performed by a commonplace girl, and *The Prime of Miss Jean
Brodie* conforms even more obediently to the requirements of
realism.

One of the connections that Muriel Spark tries to make is
between theology and aesthetics, between her beliefs and her
interest in the form of fiction, and between the truth of religion
and the kind of 'truth' that fiction is capable of communicating.
A little later one of her best critics, Frank Kermode, was to
describe her as 'so serious, so obsessed with her medium',[45] and
reading or rereading these early novels one has a strong sense of
a writer taking almost nothing for granted and prepared if
necessary to remake the art of the novel as traditionally and for
the most part currently practised. At first the preoccupation with
what the novel can be made to do lies very close, perhaps too
close, to the surface: there is something excessively pat and
schematic in Caroline Rose in *The Comforters* writing a book *on*
the novel at the same time that she is a character *in* a novel who
is involved with the composition *of* the novel. But after this
experimental first novel and the false second start represented
by *Robinson*, the novels from *Memento Mori* onwards show a
remarkable confidence and sureness of direction. Her fondness
for parodying the conventions and structures of established
modes of fiction such as the detective story and the school story
has been noted more than once, and in this respect she resembles
her contemporary, William Golding, who often uses an example
of traditional (and frequently second-rate) fiction as a starting
point for his own powerfully original works. One of the symptoms
of Muriel Spark's formal and technical concerns is her tendency
to rework themes, situations and characters from novel to novel:
while each novel is a fresh start, it often learns something from
its predecessors.

The wit and stylishness and originality of these mostly short,
highly concentrated novels won a considerable measure of
popularity for Muriel Spark; but it was a popularity that perhaps
at first did not take fully into account the subtlety of her work
or the serious nature of its intentions and implications. A few
years later, reviewing a novel in which she seemed to have made
a change of direction, *The Driver's Seat*, Frank Kermode drew
attention to the risk of underestimating her:

Henceforth, perhaps, we must not mind if her novels at first bewilder and disappoint us. We shall have to hang on to the idea that she is a much more difficult and important artist than her reputation as an entertainer has allowed many people to believe, and hope in the long run to catch up with her.[46]

This warning can be reflected back on the earlier novels, the best of which are both richly entertaining and deeply serious, approachable but subtle, readable and unpredictable.

A final element shared by these early novels is the series of heroines, from Caroline Rose and January Marlow to Jean Brodie and Joanna Childe. No mere supporting figures, they dominate, quietly or assertively, their respective novels; far from being duplicates of each other, they have in common an independence that comes from the strength of their convictions. Although these convictions may not always receive authorial endorsement, it is the same kind of independence that is displayed by the novelists, prepared to engage with the art of fiction on her own terms, to disconcert by abrupt gear-changes from realistic to fabular or allegorical modes, and to presume to explore the relationship between her own plots and God's plots for the human world.

3

Interlude

The Mandelbaum Gate (1965)

By 1963 Muriel Spark, who had been unknown as a novelist half-a-dozen years earlier, had published seven novels that had both won her a considerable reputation and caused her to be identified with a particular kind of fiction: terse, tightly constructed, often with a strong sense of period and place, but unconstrained by notions of realism and more interested in moral plotting than in psychological analysis. After *The Girls of Slender Means* her work makes a conscious change of direction: even before that novel appeared, indeed, she had begun what she described in an interview televised on 2 June 1961 as 'a new form of novel'. After some delays and some major changes of plan this became *The Mandelbaum Gate*. She seems to have found it a difficult novel to write, and it took her about two years – much longer than usual, for some of her earlier books were written within a few weeks. In its earlier form it was to have been a strongly autobiographical account of the lives of three women: herself, her mother and her grandmother. The short story 'The Gentile Jewesses', first published in 1963 and collected in *The Stories of Muriel Spark*, incorporates some of the material discarded from the novel.

The main theme of the short story is the power of narrative to conjure up something that may be indistinguishable from reality: as a child, the narrator has come to believe that she witnessed events that occurred long before her birth, so vividly have they been recounted to her by her grandmother ('What part of the scene I saw and what happened before I was born can be distinguished by my reason, but my reason cannot obliterate the scene or diminish it'). But the story also embodies

54

the theme of division, within the individual and within society, that is to be a major concern of the novel. The grandmother, who had earlier provided material for the portrayal of Louisa Jepp in *The Comforters*, is the product of a mixed marriage ('Her mother was a Gentile and her father was a Jew') and is undogmatic in her social relationships ('She was a member of the Mothers' Union of the Church of England. She attended all the social functions of the Methodists, Baptists and Quakers'), though she draws the line at Spiritualists. This division is perpetuated in the third generation, for the narrator herself is 'a Gentile Jewess like my grandmother'. The same theme is treated more seriously and at much greater length in the novel, the heroine of which is another Gentile Jewess.

Reviewing *The Mandelbaum Gate* in the *New Statesman* (15 October 1965), D. J. Enright described it as 'Mrs Spark's best, her richest and most solid novel so far'. Richness and solidity, familiar enough features of the English fictional tradition, are not qualities of this author's earlier work, and that it was possible to praise the novel in these terms suggests that it represents a deliberate turning away from her earlier manner. In another interview, published on 17 October 1965, Muriel Spark comes close to echoing Enright's words when she herself describes it as 'a very important book for me, much more concrete and solidly rooted in a very detailed setting'. Another reviewer who more explicitly applauded the change of direction was Angus Wilson, who wrote that he was

> delighted at the change and I admire her courage in making it. . . . I have increasingly felt that her books were on the edge of becoming machine-made essays in sprightly Catholic paradox. Their sheer skill and concision were hampering her development. (*Observer*, 17 October 1965)

It would not be surprising if Muriel Spark herself had felt that she could go on further in the same direction without self-imitation or self-parody; if she shared the view of many critics that *The Prime of Miss Jean Brodie* and *The Girls of Slender Means* are the finest achievements of her earlier period, she may well have decided that the time was ripe for an attempt at another kind of novel.

Many readers of *The Mandelbaum Gate*, however, are likely to

have difficulty in seeing it as 'a new form of novel'. For Ruth
Whittaker it is 'as near to a "humanist" novel as Mrs Spark ever
gets',[47] and the epithet at once links it with a central tradition
of English realist fiction. One might say that it is a novel that
could almost have been written by George Eliot – who had
shown an interest in Zionism in her last novel, *Daniel Deronda*
(1876) – if she had been writing in the 1970s instead of a hundred
years earlier. There are also some striking similarities with the
most important novel of another 'humanist' novelist, E. M.
Forster: like *A Passage to India*, *The Mandelbaum Gate* has a heroine
who goes abroad to find the man she intends to marry (while at
the same time having some reservations about the marriage); it
deals with the collision of cultures and religions; and it explores
the problems of friendship and of wholeness within the individual
personality. Another major character, Freddy Hamilton, is a
very Forsterian figure: like, for example, Philip Herriton in *Where
Angels Fear to Tread*, Freddy is trapped within the rigid code of
behaviour of the English middle class and the public schools,
and dominated by a tyrannical mother, but enabled in a foreign
setting to actualise latent and repressed elements in his own
nature.

As these comments suggest, *The Mandelbaum Gate* is a novel of
'character' in a sense in which none of its seven predecessors
can be said to be. In the terms made famous by Forster in his
Aspects of the Novel, Freddy begins as a 'flat' character, almost a
caricature, but shows himself later to be capable of 'roundness'
as unsuspected areas of his nature surface in speech and action.
There are even passages in the novel that read like parodies of
the kind of character-sketch that is standard practice in Victorian
and Edwardian fiction. Of Ãbdul Ramdez, for instance:

> The facts are as follows. He was born in 1927 at the small
> and ancient town of Madaba in the Transjordan, east of the
> Dead Sea. He had three sisters, four half-sisters, and one
> brother. At that time the family consisted of his father, an
> unmarried uncle, Joe Ramdez's first wife, who acted as general
> manager of domestic life, a second wife (Adbul's mother), who
> looked after all the younger children. . . . (1965 edition, p. 94)

– and much more in similar vein. This kind of 'solidity of

specification' (in Henry James's phrase) is hardly to be found in the earlier novels.

Character is important in *The Mandelbaum Gate* because the emphasis in this novel falls not (as so often earlier) on fabular or allegorical patterns in which the individuals involved are little more than ciphers, but on the insights afforded by individual experience, the workings of individual conscience, and the attainment of individual wholeness of being. In contrast to the individual stand groups, clans and categories of all kinds: racial, religious, of nation or class or language. Peter Kemp's useful commentary on the novel emphasises this aspect:

> The novel swarms with instances of people believing what they want to believe, thinking in terms of type not person, the species rather than the individual, and then going on to regard these different groups or categories as alien, potentially or actual hostile. . . . Variously mocking intense commitment to a party or a group, the novel is far from deriding intensity itself. What it advocates is not a tepid caution, low-pressure existence, non-involvement, chary drawing-back from life. On the contrary, and with considerable eloquence, it urges involvement and concern, but channelled always towards the individual, not towards the clan.[48]

A corollary of this is that 'simple allegiance to a group or code must entail the suppression of some areas of personality',[49] and this generalisation is worked out concretely and dramatically through the two main characters, Barbara and Freddy. As Barbara says at one point, ' "There's always more to it than Jew, Gentile, half-Jew, half-Gentile. There's the human soul, the individual. . . . Something unique and unrepeatable" '.

Reduced to the simplest terms, the theme of the novel is, as Ruth Whittaker says, 'division and the means of unity',[50] and the Mandelbaum Gate is the central symbol, dividing the holy city of Jerusalem into two political parts. The intricate plot and the lavish provision of circumstantial details in this, the longest of all Muriel Spark's books, exhibit these preoccupations with division and unity at many levels. The Middle East setting (Muriel Spark spent two months in Israel in 1961), in which the holy places of Christendom are separated by political barriers, offers a contemporary case-study of the evils of division. The

heroine, Barbara Vaughan, is on a pilgrimage to the Christian
shrines and risks danger by crossing and recrossing the frontier;
she is also divided in her origins, being a half-Jewish convert to
Roman Catholicism. Barbara's experience teaches her that
placing people in categories leads to grievous errors of judgement
(and we may note again that this is a favourite theme of the
traditional English novel from Jane Austen onwards): thus, after
rejecting a relationship, perhaps unconsciously lesbian, with a
fellow schoolmistress because it is based on a false assumption
about the kind of person she herself really is, she is further
enlightened to find the prim and spinsterish Miss Rickward
surrendering to passion and marriage against all expectations.

But, as Peter Kemp reminds us, to reject categories and
divisions does not mean the acceptance of a bland and universally
accommodating attitude, and a key text for this novel is a verse
from the Apocalypse first quoted by Barbara at the end of
Chapter 1:

> I know of thy doings, and find thee neither cold nor hot; cold
> or hot, I would thou wert one or the other. Being what thou
> art, lukewarm, neither cold nor hot, thou wilt make me vomit
> thee out of my mouth.

This lukewarm or Laodicean attitude (see *Revelation* 3: 14–18) is
initially exemplified by Freddy, at whom Barbara's quotation is
directed, and who regards her words as in very poor taste
('Freddy did not reply. People should definitely not quote the
Scriptures at one. It was quite absurd': p. 16); but Freddy's own
life, and his sense of self, undergo a profound upheaval in the
course of the story, and he later appropriates the text for his
own use.

As a diplomat Freddy can cross and recross the border without
difficulty, but at the outset he takes with him, like an extra skin,
his own essential Englishness: he notes with approval that
English wildflowers, their seeds scattered by visitors, flourish in
the Holy Land, and he enjoys a tea party in the garden as if it
were a summer's day in England. Significantly, he enjoys writing
occasional verse in difficult metrical forms that seem to symbolise
the rigidly ordered and predictable nature of his existence. Yet
even Freddy, who has constructed a tolerable lifestyle out of
barriers and divisions that keep at bay the unfamiliar and the

risky, is involved in a thriller-like escapade that remakes his personality – or, more exactly, opens up neglected and suppressed areas. By a nice touch the most shocking incident in the book comes from the least expected quarter: Freddy's mother, living in the genteel town of Harrogate, is murdered by her companion, as if to demonstrate that one ought not to assume that life will conform to categories, even such apparently unassailable categories as English watering-places and middle-class gentle-women.

As Barbara says to Suzi at one point, ' "There's a curious change come over Freddy" ' (p. 251), and Freddy's 'conversion', to use the term loosely, is one of the most interesting elements in the book. It might almost be said to be *too* interesting, for there is a sense in which Freddy competes with Barbara for centrality: there are stretches in which we hear little or nothing of her, and his gradual recovery of memory of what has happened during the 'missing' period accounts for a large part of the narrative interest of the second half of the novel, which is recounted through a series of time shifts that partly mirror Freddy's stage-by-stage victory over his amnesia. But there is ultimately no competition between the two characters, for they travel, from very different starting points and by different roads, to a similar destination and represent the working out of a common theme.

The richness and solidity of the novel no doubt owe something to its autobiographical origins and to the visit to Israel already referred to. There is a strong sense of place, and of the differences between places. At a distance, remote from the action but strong in the mental lives of the characters, is England: not, this time, the raffish and socially mixed England of the earlier novels, but a middle-class – one might say a Forsterian – England of public schools and private schools, gentlemen's clubs and elderly ladies living on their dividends. Close at hand is the strife-torn Middle East, especially Israel and Jordan, created with scrupulous attention to geography and topography, to architecture and flora, houses and furniture, food and drink and costume. The time scheme too is very precise, both internally and in relation to actual public events. At the outset (p. 4) we learn that it is 1961, the year in which the author visited Israel and also the year of the trial of Adolf Eichmann (on p. 105, 1961 is referred to as 'the year of the Eichmann trial'). Barbara disappears on

12 August 1961 (p. 117), and from this point the events are
recounted in considerable detail: although the time shifts rule
out a diary effect, by the end we have been given a day-by-day
and almost an hour-by-hour account of the adventures of Barbara
and Freddy.

For much of the novel an omniscient narrator seems to be
firmly in charge, and a sentence such as the following, assured
in its sweeping generalisation, could have been written by
Forster: 'The ideal reposed in their religion, but somewhere in
the long trail of Islam, the knack of disinterestedness had been
lost, and with it a large portion of the joy of life' (p. 90). With
the time shifts of the latter part of the narrative, however, a more
subjective and more impressionistic – more Conradian – mode
seems to operate as various characters try to make sense of their
experiences (Freddy, most notably, struggling to comprehend
what has happened to him), and Part II opens (p. 205) with a
Proustian tribute to the individuality of memory:

> Freddy Hamilton, Barbara Vaughan, Suzi Ramdez – each, in
> later years, when they looked back on that time, remembered
> one particular event before all others. It was different in each
> case. Alexandros, too, had his special recollection that was to
> gleam suddenly. . . .

'In later years', incidentally, seems an odd phrase in a narrative
whose events predate publication by only four years, but this is
not the only point at which the narrator looks forward to a future
that is part of the reader's future (cf. '. . . those years after Joe
Ramdez's death in 1963 . . .' p. 266, and elsewhere).

The Mandelbaum Gate is a good novel but not a typical one, its
strengths lying partly, even substantially, in areas that the author
had not previously explored and in which she was to show little
subsequent interest. It works well as a novel of character, and
especially as that familiar kind of fictional project, the exploration
of the ways in which encountering unfamiliar circumstances
opens up new areas of personality and new capacities for
relationships. But it shows little of Muriel Spark's characteristic
interest in her medium and in the nature of fictionality (there is
a passing reference to Barbara's state of mind as resembling
'that [which] the anti-novelists induce': p. 187). In the event it

seems to have been a disappointment to its author, who declared in a 1970 interview:

> I don't like that book awfully much. . . . It's out of proportion. In the beginning it's slow, and the end is very rapid. . . . I got bored because it was too long, so I decided never again to write a long book. Keep them very short.

She has stuck to that resolve, and the change of direction that *The Mandelbaum Gate* seemed to signal has turned out to be only a detour or blind alley.

At the same time the novel's argument is one that lies very close to the heart of Muriel Spark's moral position, and she powerfully endorses the heroine's rejection of divisive categories (represented most painfully by the choric background of the trial of Eichmann, an instrument in an ideological and political programme that sought to destroy an entire human group) and her quest for wholeness. This comes out most clearly and eloquently in a passage near the end of the novel, where Barbara answers Suzi's question about her sincerity:

> 'Are you sincere in these devotions, when you go to them talking and laughing with me so much about love-affairs and men and sex? Oh, Barbara, I don't mean that you're not sincere, as I like it so much when everything can be said.'
> 'Well, either religious faith penetrates everything in life or it doesn't. There are some experiences that seem to make nonsense of all separations of sacred from profane – they seem childish. Either the whole of life is unified under God or everything falls apart. Sex is child's play in the argument.'
> (pp. 307–8)

The refusal to separate sacred from profane, here made explicit, is characteristic of much of Muriel Spark's best work and responsible both for its distinctively elusive tone and for a tendency on the part of some critics and readers to take its apparent lightness at face value.

Patricia Stubbs's severe judgement on *The Mandelbaum Gate* is that 'This novel is still marred by Miss Spark's intermittent refusal to apply reason to her fictional situations, her propensity to dwell on the absurd and ironic for their own sake'.[51] To

demand reason of one who has never pretended to be a rationalist
seems unreasonable; but in any case an explicit and recurrent
theme of the novel is that 'With God all things are possible'.
The unexpected takes many forms: Freddy compels the reader
to revise a confident placing of him as a familiar type of fussy
bachelor, nervous of experience; bloody violence bursts upon the
outward decorum of Harrogate; Miss Rickward, apparently a
man-hater, is startlingly and ludicrously found in bed with an
elderly Arab. Reason is a poor guide to a world in which such
things can happen: this is not a dwelling upon 'the absurd and
ironic for their own sake', but an insistence that this is what the
world is like, outside as well as within the novel.

As novel-critics, moreover, we may prefer to deal with the
kind of fiction that leaves us with no unresolved puzzles or
inexplicable mysteries on our hands, but as novel-readers we
should be ready, as Keats says of the poet, to rest in uncertainties
with no irritable striving after fact and reason. As Barbara
Vaughan reflects near the end of the novel, 'Knots were not
necessarily created to be untied. Questions were things that
sufficed in their still beauty, answering themselves' (pp. 301–2).
Muriel Spark, like the Forster of *A Passage to India*, is under no
contract to offer the reader a novel that can be cracked like a
code or a nut: the solution of a code and the kernel of a nut are
limited things, whereas novels like these can convey the mystery
and the endless possibilities of life itself.

In an unobtrusively important passage of *The Mandelbaum Gate*,
Muriel Spark writes:

> To Barbara, one of the first attractions of her religion's moral
> philosophy had been its recognition of the helpless complexity
> of motives that prompted an action, and its consequent
> emphasis on actual words, thoughts and deeds; there was
> seldom one motive only in the grown person; the main thing
> was that motives should harmonize. Ricky did not understand
> harmony as an ideal in this sense. She assumed that it was
> both right that people should tear themselves to bits about
> their motives and possible for them to make up their minds
> what their motives were. Herein, Barbara reflected, lies the
> difficulty in dealing with Ricky. . . . (pp. 169–70)

The novel as a literary genre, recognising 'the helpless complexity of motives', emphasises 'actual words, thoughts and deeds' in its attempt to achieve harmony, whereas criticism, like Miss Rickward, too often tries to define, to simplify, and to tidy up. Oddly enough, though, after *The Mandelbaum Gate* Muriel Spark turns to a kind of fiction that is very little concerned with motivation and which, rather than seeking to harmonise, depicts a world of fragmented existences and of public and private violence. From the richness and complexity of *The Mandelbaum Gate* she turns back to the self-denying spareness of the novella; whereas the early novellas, though, had often lovingly recreated a past observed with humour, the later ones are set in a contemporary and cosmopolitan world that is as hard and shiny, and apparently as unfeeling, as plastic.

4
Foreign Parts: The Later Novels

The Public Image (1968); *The Driver's Seat* (1970); *Not to Disturb* (1971); *The Hothouse by the East River* (1973); *The Abbess of Crewe* (1974); *The Takeover* (1976); *Territorial Rights* (1979); *Loitering with Intent* (1981); *The Only Problem* (1984)

Having settled in Rome in 1966, Muriel Spark published two years later the first of her Italian novels, *The Public Image*. Its world is a hard contemporary one of film studios, sensational journalism, and international celebrities, and it is partly (though not primarily) a satire on the media industry and the fictions generated by its highly efficient and totally unscrupulous publicity machine. Its central concerns are ones familiar to readers of the earlier novels: the relationship of truth to fiction, of character and identity to 'personality' and 'image', of life's plots to the plots of the novelist.

The heroine, Annabel, is an actress of apparently limited ability who is transformed into a star by the skill and dedication of the professional film-makers. The publisher's blurb on the jacket of the first edition describes her as 'enchanting', but this seems hardly the *mot juste* for one whose looks, intelligence and personality are of a decidedly commonplace order. Early in the novel the narrator describes her uncompromisingly as 'stupid' (p. 13 in the 1968 Macmillan edition, to which all future references apply), and observes that she is 'unaccustomed to organise anything', but she develops in the course of the story and emerges as calculating but resourceful in ensuring her survival in a glamorous world that turns out to be a kind of jungle. One of the problems explored is the measures to which a woman may be driven in an exploitative world. But the main point about Annabel is the difference between her public image and the reality that lies behind it – a question complicated by the fact that the image is itself threatened with destruction and the reality undergoes a change.

As an actress Annabel is, like many another Spark heroine, a maker of fictions, or at least an abetter in their making. But the situation is more complicated than this, for the 'real' Annabel (who is, of course, a fiction of Muriel Spark's) is presented to the public not only in her confessedly fictional roles (the parts she plays in films) but in a much-publicised version of her private self that is, as it happens, also a fiction. The studio publicity has created an image for her that is itself actually two images: of a woman cool, elegant and controlled in the daytime who after dark is fiercely sensual within the confines of her marriage. Among all these Annabels, which one is real?

But even this does not exhaust the list, for another image is devised for her by her husband as his dying act. An unsuccessful actor whose career has fallen behind hers, he commits suicide after writing a number of letters – to their child, his mother (who has long been dead herself), and others – designed to vilify Annabel's reputation and destroy her career. In terms calculated to make a strong appeal to the popular press, she is accused of holding orgies, and he even arranges matters so that at the time of his death she will (to her own bewilderment) appear to be giving a wild party. As Annabel says when she hears the contents of the letters, ' "He's done it just like the journalists do when they want to cook up a scandal. I hear they even invent letters" ' (p. 135). His allegations are a pack of lies, but on the other hand he is merely replacing one fiction with another (a former screen-writer, he has made the letters his last work of fiction): in a world divorced from reality fictions propagate other fictions. To a credulous and eager public, however, with a keener appetite for vivid fictions than for commonplace truths, these fictions will be equally accepted as reality: as a character says, ' "It's what they want to believe that counts" ' (p. 126).

The phrase 'public image' haunts the novel, which is domi-nated by attempts to create, modify, destroy and salvage (and, finally, abandon) Annabel's image. It will not quite do, however, to make a simple distinction between truth and fiction, the reality and the image, for people can grow into their images. As a film

director tells her, ' "Life is all the achievement of an effect. Only
the animals remain natural" ', and he counters her naive protests
that the image foisted on her does not represent her real self:

> 'But I'm not a Tiger-Lady,' she said.
> 'Aren't you? Come and live a little with me and you soon
> will be.'
> 'I doubt it.'
> 'Before I made you the Tiger-Lady, you didn't even look
> like a lady in public, never mind a tiger in private. It's what
> I began to make of you that you've partly become.' (p. 52)

The first half of the novel moves rather slowly, but after the
husband's suicide at the mid-point it gains in speed and intensity.
Annabel's marriage has been a tame affair, with a waning of
interest in sex, a drifting apart and a listless consideration of
divorce or separation (all this of course very different from the
public image of the devoted couple decorous in public, but
enjoying a rich and full physical relationship in private); but the
realisation that she has become the victim of her husband's plot
and the threat to her career bring out qualities in her that have
not been previously evident. Quickly rallying, she proceeds to
invent fictions of her own: by playing the part of a grieving
widow, forgiving the women who have supposedly pestered her
dead husband with their attentions, gathering her neighbours
around her in a carefully staged scene, and handling the media
with great skill.

A further threat to her security then presents itself in the
unattractive shape of her pretended friend Billy, a blackmailer.
The attempted blackmail near the end of the book is fore-
shadowed by a simile used very near the beginning:

> Billy was like a worn-out something that one had bought years
> ago on the hire-purchase system, and was still paying up with
> no end to it in sight. And again, Billy treated her newly-
> sprouting film success as a win on the football-pools (p. 9)

– the kind of detail, apparently self-indulgent, but actually highly
functional, that is characteristic of this closely woven, highly
organised novel. Annabel takes up the challenge and for the first
time acts like a free individual: in a final reversal she breaks

through the web of pretence and deceit and leaves the country with the baby that has all along been her only link with genuine human feeling, 'the only reality of her life' (p. 53).

At the end of the novel Annabel has shed her images and is simply a woman with a baby, no longer recognised as a famous film star by the passing crowds at the airport:

> Waiting for the order to board, she felt both free and unfree. The heavy weight of the bags was gone; she felt as if she was still, curiously, pregnant with the baby, but not pregnant in fact. She was pale as a shell. She did not wear her dark glasses. Nobody recognised her as she stood, having moved the baby to rest on her hip, conscious also of the baby in a sense weightlessly and perpetually within her, as an empty shell contains, by its very structure, the echo and harking image of former and former seas.

The final lyricism is by now a familiar feature of a Muriel Spark novel, but the shell also harks back to an earlier disparaging reference to Annabel as being like an empty shell. She is 'both free and unfree', the normal condition of ordinary humanity, and it cannot be said that she has enjoyed such freedom at any earlier point in the story. Her moral growth is genuine and, in the novel, unique: the shedding of her dark glasses is surely symbolic.

In walking out of her career and leaving behind the roles or images that have fettered her freedom, Annabel has also walked out of the world of men, for it is noteworthy that the male characters have in their different ways manipulated her for their own purposes: the film director for his professional success, her husband in gratifying his envy and longing for revenge, Billy as a source of free meals and, later, blackmail payments. The infernal chorus of journalists and media-people is also predominantly male, and it is only by turning her back on this male world, ever ready to exploit her, that she can realise her selfhood.

Its interest in the nature of fictions and their relationship to reality links *The Public Image* with Muriel Spark's first novel, *The Comforters*, as well as with some of the novels that came between them. But the differences are more striking than the resemblances, and one has a sense of this novel as an experiment of a different kind and a very conscious turning in a new direction. Its most obvious feature is what it omits or eschews. Ruth Whittaker finds it 'unique amongst Mrs Spark's novels in its strong endorsement of instinctive action not finally contained within a religious framework',[52] and the absence of a theological context for human action gives it a barer, less resonant quality that is matched by the anonymity of the settings and the shallowness of most of the characters. Gone are the remembered worlds of London and Edinburgh, recreated in careful and perhaps affectionate detail and with an evident relish for the quiddities of locale and period. In their place is a cosmopolitan, impersonal and indifferent world of the rich, the ambitious and the rootless: the setting is Rome, but could equally well be Paris or New York or Los Angeles. As in many of the novels that followed it, *The Public Image* seems to present a world only partly furnished with the objects that in the traditional novel offer an assurance of solid reality.

Equally spare and unornamented is the book's structure: as Peter Kemp says, the novel is 'undeviatingly devoted to a single chain-reaction of hate, envy, and deception'.[53] With such a programme, it could hardly be anything other than serious, and along with so much else Muriel Spark now seems to have left behind the humour (ranging in its varieties from wit to farce) and the good-humoured pleasure in the oddity of the world and its inhabitants that give such a distinctive tone to a novel like *Memento Mori*. It is almost as if an attempt were being made to reduce a novel, or 'the novel', to its barest essentials.

For Peter Kemp, this experiment has negative results: 'Dramatically jettisoning inessentials in [*The Public Image*],' he writes, Mrs Spark seems unsure what to do with the space she has created'.[54] This criticism has been countered by Malcolm Bradbury:

... Muriel Spark's [novels] are end-directed; no author could be surer about where things are going. From her novels the beginning, which creates expectation and freedom, and the middle, which substantiates and qualifies it, seem absent. Her people arise at the last, *from* the last; what has withered is a world of motive, purpose, aspiration. The curious inescapability of plot is her subject, in some real sense her satisfaction. Compared with James, she has nothing to offer about the significance of impressions, the taking in of experience, the value of the vaunted scene, and there is no substantial self to be made from apprehending the contingencies of experience. In that way her work conveys significant absences, a feeling of omission, and so has considerable resemblances to a good deal of contemporary art, including the *nouveau roman*. In the end, it seems finally to deny the notion of personal authenticity out of which humanists, gently, and existentialists, assertively, make character.

'The essence of the art,' Bradbury argues, 'is its hardness'.[55] There could hardly be a better example of the 'end-directed' novel than *The Driver's Seat*, which pushes still further the experiment begun in *The Public Image*. Even by this author's normally succinct standards, this is a very short novel, running to barely one hundred pages of large type, and along with this brevity goes a high degree of concentration, a density of effect in which slight shifts of style, small repetitions, apparently trivial details, all assume significance. Nothing is artistically superfluous or gratuitous, nothing included simply to convey the impression of a well-stocked, fully furnished fictional world that has a reassuring resemblance to the one we inhabit. Much of the action takes place in public buildings such as airport terminals and department stores, or in more private locations such as hotel bedrooms which still bear little imprint of individual human personality. This total rejection of the pathetic fallacy and insistence on the indifference of the external world is one aspect of an all-pervading coldness, objectivity, 'hardness' and even heartlessness in the narrative tone and method – aesthetic and formal qualities that mirror the inhumanity and indifference of the contemporary world. For this is, like its predecessor, a tale of rootless existences in cosmopolitan settings – the clean well-lighted places of advertisements in magazines.

For human beings to behave with inhumanity is, by definition, unnatural, and unnaturalness is a central theme in this novel, taking many forms from references to synthetic materials such as plastics to unpredictable and violent language and behaviour. In the opening episode, the protagonist, Lise, is buying a dress to wear on the vacation that starts the next day and is offered one of stain-resistant man-made material. It is the first object to be named in a book in which objects are to play an important part, not because of their intimate attachment to personality but because of their otherness, their alien detachment from human existence and emotion. Lise rejects the dress with an explosion of anger, insisting that she wants one that *will* show stains. The reaction is the first in a series of sudden, startling, eccentric and unexplained acts that draw attention to her, and also her first step in laying a trail that is to determine her every act.

One of the oldest kinds of story is that involving a quest, and this is precisely what Lise undertakes: she says at one point that she is travelling to a foreign city to 'find' a boyfriend – not to meet or join or pick up one, but to find one. The object of her quest is in fact her own murderer, and her journey ends in what amounts to a planned act of self-destruction: in a reversal of the pattern familiar both in reality and in realistic fiction, she is a victim in search of a murderer.[56] Once again Muriel Spark's starting point seems to be varieties of popular fiction that offer palatable, but usually false, versions of reality. A familiar type of magazine story is that in which the heroine, while on holiday in some exotic spot, enters into a romantic relationship; and *The Driver's Seat* parodies such optimistic tales by showing the protagonist in quest of a lover, rejecting various candidates on the grounds that they are 'not my type' (a recurring phrase), and finally selecting a reluctant partner who becomes both her victim and her murderer.

At the same time the novel is an inverted version of the traditional detective story (parodied earlier in *Memento Mori*): here the victim selects, pursues and corners the killer, in the process deliberately laying a trail (normally the unconscious and unintended role of the criminal) which the police will subsequently follow. The detective story exhibits in a specialised form the normal concern of traditional fiction with cause and effect; this time such a relationship seems, like so much else in this story, to be reversed, just as the crime comes at the end rather than, as in most detective fiction, near the beginning. This is therefore not a 'whodunnit' but, to use a term that appears in the novel, a 'whydunnit', and what remains obscure (though guessable) is the motivation with which, again, traditional fiction is so largely occupied. (The novelist–protagonist of a later novel, *Loitering with Intent*, remarks at one point that she 'didn't go in for motives, I never have'). These are only some of the ways in which *The Driver's Seat*, while apparently imitating or alluding to established kinds of fiction, rejects most of the traditional assumptions concerning the business of the novel.

An outline of the story will illustrate some of these features in a narrative that is written with crisp lucidity and presents a strong and easily grasped sequence of events, but which at many points displays cracks or fissures in the realistic surface and baffles the expectations of a reader nourished on traditions of fictional realism.

The opening line of the novel is in the present tense, and, apart from some brief excursions into the future tense that will be referred to later, this is maintained consistently throughout. Most narratives employ a past tense that endows the action, however vividly dramatic it may seem as it unfolds, with a shaped and determined quality and enables the narrator to speak with authority. (There are some exceptions, even in nineteenth-century fiction, such as the third-person narrative that occupies about half of Dickens's *Bleak House*, and occasional, much briefer present-tense passages in Charlotte Brontë's *Jane Eyre*, but these are striking and memorable effects because they are departures from the general rule.) In much of this novel nothing seems to be known until it is stated, and the effect is of an open-ended narrative in which the totally unexpected can suddenly happen – as indeed it often does. But paradoxically the conclusion is predetermined ('end-directed'), and the closing words of the novel, the Aristotelian phrase 'pity and fear', remind us that this is a tragedy on classical lines in which, whatever may happen on the way, the only destinationn can be the death of the protagonist.

In the department store in which the story opens, Lise rejects the stain-resistant dress; having moved on to another store, she then selects and purchases a dress and coat that are individually lurid and, worn together, clash hideously in colour and design. It is as if she is trying to draw attention to herself, both by her behaviour to the sales assistants and by choosing these startlingly unsuitable clothes to wear. Their design is geometrical: the dress has 'bright V's of orange, mauve and blue', the coat 'narrow stripes, red and white' (Penguin edition, 1974, pp. 10–11), just as the dress that she originally chose was 'patterned with green and purple squares on a white background' (p. 7). As in the description a little later of Lise's one-room flat, with its severe lines and absence of anything giving individuality, the suggestion is of a mathematical, mechanical precision that excludes the spontaneous and subdues the natural. This becomes explicit at the end of the description of the flat, where the prize-winning designer has used pinewood extensively and 'The swaying tall pines among the litter of cones on the forest floor have been subdued into silence and into obedient bulks' (p. 15). Lise's lips are 'normally pressed together like the ruled line of a balance sheet' (p. 9) – another rejection of the natural and spontaneous; and the simile is not chosen at random, for she works in an accountant's office, where she has, with rigid symmetry, 'five girls under her and two men', while 'Over her are two women and five men'. All of this helps to form part of one of the central patterns of the novel, the tension between the fortuitous, unplanned quality of life (such as the chance acquaintances encountered on a journey or in a hotel) and the relentless, obsessive, monomaniacal purpose by which Lise is driven (or, more exactly, drives) to her destiny.

At the end of the opening chapter Lise promises to leave some car keys for a friend while she is on holiday, but in the event fails to do so. In the second chapter the scene shifts to the airport, where again she behaves eccentrically, in a manner calculated to ensure that she is not easily forgotten, at the check-in counter. Throughout the novel she complains, quarrels, speaks more loudly than is normal, laughs hysterically, bursts into tears, stares at strangers; and this behaviour is both evidence of her serious mental instability (there is a hint that she had a breakdown five years earlier) and part of the elaborate trail she is laying. At the airport it is 'almost as if, satisfied that she has successfully registered the fact of her presence . . . among the July thousands there, she has fulfilled a small item of a greater purpose' (p. 20): and here again we detect a reversal of the usual fictional situation, where greater purposes are the business of the novelist and not the characters. Lise is the spinner of her own plot, a very active and purposeful victim hunting a passive and reluctant murderer. Before she boards the plane, she examines, but does not purchase, a paper-knife at the airport shop.

We learn in this chapter that she is travelling south, but neither her place of departure nor her destination is named. From various hints, however, it emerges that she is going from Copenhagen to Rome; but at first it is merely a journey from a city 'in the North' to 'a foreign city' in the south. Nor is there any hint of the period in which the action is set, though it appears to be in the present day. We are not even told Lise's surname, and many of the characters are never named at all. This indifference to specificity once more seems like a rejection of what has normally been held dear by the traditional novel, which often begins by establishing times, places and genealogies in some detail. On the other hand there is an explicit time scheme relating to the very short period (less than two days) covered by the action. And, perhaps puzzlingly, we are treated to meticulous descriptions of things apparently of very little importance: the snack served during the flight, for instance, is itemised with great precision. Much detailed information is furnished concerning trivial matters – we are told several times that Lise departs from Gate 14 at the airport – and commonplace objects and processes are evoked with fastidious precision:

> She opens her suitcase and carefully extracts a short dressing-gown. She takes out a dress, hangs it in the cupboard, takes it off the hanger again, folds it neatly and puts it back. She takes out her sponge-bag and bedroom slippers, undresses, put on her dressing-gown and goes into the bathroom, shutting the door. (p. 47)

The lack of syntactical variety is deliberate, as is the avoidance of epithets suggesting a sensuous response: it is a clinical world without colour or texture, and there is something robot-like about Lise's movements. Even her neatness seems a compulsion rather than a virtue.

Muriel Spark here seems to be following writers of the French 'nouveau roman' such as Alain Robbe-Grillet, who conceived the role of fiction as the dispassionate description of the external world as a substitute for the traditional novel's concern with character. And such passages reinforce the vision of the world she presents in this novel, a world without attachments, loyalties, or stable relationships: the characters in *The Driver's Seat* are foreign tourists whose transitory contacts are with waiters, hotel clerks, taxi-drivers, sales assistants. There is no sense of home or even of a mother tongue in this rootless, polyglot society; and although Lise refers sometimes to her family it is clearly non-existent, a fantasy entertained by someone unloving and unloved. Where Muriel Spark most obviously differs from the writers of the 'new novel' is in the occasional lyricism (as in 'The swaying tall pines . . .' quoted earlier) and the touches of humour, as in the second half of a sentence that begins in irreproachably objective terms:

> She switches on the central light which is encased in a mottled glass globe; the light flicks on, then immediately flickers out as if, having served a long succession of clients without complaint, Lise is suddenly too much for it. (p. 45)

The other point to note about the second chapter is that it introduces the first two examples of a device that occurs (on my count) nine times in the course of the novel: the brief switch from the present to the future tense as the reader is given a glimpse of what will happen after the end of the book. It is as if there were a temporary gap in the curtain that separates man from his fate. The first example is startling: in the course of the description of Lise at the beginning of Chapter 2 we read that

> She is neither good-looking nor bad-looking. Her nose is short and wider than it will look in the likeness constructed partly by the method of identikit, partly by actual photography, soon to be published in the newspapers of four languages (p. 18)

and subsequent flashforwards both prefigure and make inevitable the end of the story and sketch the outline of events after the conclusion of the narrative.

The third chapter recounts Lise's journey and arrival at her destination. In the queue to board the aircraft she has 'chosen' a fellow passenger, a young man, 'to adhere to', and has herself been picked out by another young man who is following her. On board they occupy a group of three seats, with Lise in the middle: another symmetrical patterning. The man she has picked out from the crowd 'stares, as if recognizing her' though in fact he has never seen her before; before take-off he moves away in panic, 'as if he had escaped from death by a small margin', and occupies another seat. The other man, who turns out to be an advocate for 'natural' foods (and a satire on one form of contemporary obsession with what is supposed to be natural), flirts with her.

When they arrive, Lise accosts an elderly man who has sat behind her: she feels sure that he is the one she has come to meet, and bursts into tears when she turns out to be wrong. She arranges to meet the younger man at his hotel at seven o'clock.

In Chapter 4, having reached her hotel room, she again draws attention to herself by loud complaints. She also studies a map of the city and 'marks a spot in a large patch of green, the main parkland of the city'; beside a building marked as 'The Pavilion' she puts a cross. Going out, she meets a fellow guest, Mrs Fiedke, an elderly Canadian widow; they share a taxi and Lise stuffs her passport down the back of the seat and leaves it there. One has a sense that she is not only making preparations for what is to come, but shedding the appurtenances of her former life as if she will no longer have any use for them. It is rather as if Sophocles' and Anouilh's Antigone were to give away her belongings before going out to bury her brother and encompass her own death.

Mrs Fiedke tells Lise that her nephew is arriving that evening from Copenhagen (a city now mentioned for the first time); he should have arrived by now but has, she says, missed the plane (presumably the one Lise was on). His name is Richard and he has been 'unwell' (there is a hint of mental disturbance). Lise tells her that she has 'to meet a friend', also that she can drive. They go shopping together and Lise buys an odd assortment of articles: two scarves, a couple of black ties, a cheap food-blender, a plastic bag; for the department store, like the world outside (and like that world's human population), is full of objects existing separately and in indifference to each other. The old lady buys a pair of slippers for her nephew, also a paper-knife, putting the latter into Lise's bag; later she finds she has lost the slippers, which later still also turn up in Lise's bag. (In Freudian terms the slippers and knife are obvious symbols for, respectively, the female and male genitalia, hinting at the final rape.)

Chapter 5 shows the two women still exploring Rome together. Mrs Fiedke, who seems on the verge of senility, tells Lise that she and her nephew are 'made for each other' – a romantic cliché that has a significance of which she is unaware. (Any cliché used by Muriel Spark is apt to carry more than its usual modest weight of meaning.) They are caught up in a demonstration in which students clash with police and tear-gas is used – a reminder of the public violence of contemporary Europe – and they are separated. Lise takes refuge in a garage and meets the proprietor, Carlo, who tries unsuccessfully to remove a grease stain that has marked her coat. She tells him, untruthfully, that she is staying at the Hilton and he offers to drive her there; but on the way makes sexual advances which she rejects, and she seizes the opportunity to drive off without him. At the Hilton she sees a wealthy Arab emerging, surrounded by his retinue; later she learns that he is a potentate in whose absence from his country there has been a coup. Inside, she meets the old man from the plane, an English aristocrat who has been at school with the Arab. In the washroom she leaves behind the bunch of keys she has brought from home, with the remark that she 'won't be wanting these now'.

When she emerges from the hotel, she finds that Carlo has driven off his car; her occupancy of the driver's seat on this occasion was only temporary. She already knows that the old man is not the one she is looking for, and she has told Carlo that he is 'not my type'; so her quest continues. She is still engaged in drawing attention to herself as often as possible (exactly the reverse of the behaviour of most active partners in a homicidal relationship) – for example, by a bizarre conversation with a policeman, and by throwing Carlo's keys out of the window of her taxi. We learn that all the strangers she encounters separately and randomly, though unknown to each other, will be united as 'witnesses' when enquiries are made into her murder.

By now it is evening, and in Chapter 6 she arrives at the Metropole to meet Bill, the macrobiological food fanatic from the plane. In his car they drive to the Pavilion, an old villa in a park (already marked on the city map by Lise). Bill's intentions, like Carlo's, are sexual, but she raises an outcry and drives off, leaving him to be arrested.

Returning to her hotel, in the final chapter she finds at the reception desk a young man who has just arrived. It becomes clear that he is Mrs Fiedke's nephew; also that he is the young man who changed his seat to avoid her on the flight. She tells him, 'You're coming with me', and tells the porter that he can keep the man's luggage: he too, it seems, is moving towards the point at which he will no longer need possessions. We are told that he did not, as his aunt supposed, miss the plane, but came to the hotel earlier in the day and, seeing Lise, left in haste. But this second attempt to escape his destiny is no more successful than the first; and, telling him 'I've been looking for you all day', Lise leads him to the car, and sits in the driver's seat.

In the course of their conversation it emerges that he has been in prison and in a mental home after stabbing a woman, and Lise tells him that women get killed 'because they want to be'. In the park again, she gives him the paper-knife and scarves, tells him precisely what to do, lies down, and is then bound and killed by him – though not quite in accordance with her instructions.

As this somewhat extended commentary on a work hardly longer than many short stories may suggest, *The Driver's Seat* is a text that combines the kind of singleness of action that Aristotle thought proper to tragedy with an abundance of local detail and incident, some of it (for example, the Arab who comes out of the hotel) far from obvious in its purpose. The narrative moves in a single straight line as Lise makes the preparations for her journey, travels to the foreign city, finds the man she is looking for, and dies. But it also accommodates much that seems random, arbitrary, perhaps irrelevant. This combination of opposite qualities gives the story tension by pulling it in two ways, and seems to reflect the novelist's vision of a life that may seem contingent, aimless, unpredictable, but may also have a hidden purpose and a high degree of patterning whereby one apparently insignificant detail acquires meaning through its relationship with others.

One example of this is the use of numbers, which appear prominently but for the most part gratuitously in this novel – or so it would at first appear. On closer inspection we find that certain numbers, especially the traditionally powerful, even magical, numbers three and seven (and their compounds), appear more often than chance would seem to dictate. As we have seen, on the plane Lise sits in the middle of a group of three seats; this pattern is exactly repeated later, in the hotel washroom, where she stands at the wash-basin between two other women, and once again when the Arab leaving the Hilton is flanked by two men in business suits. In the hotel room are three bell-pushes; a night-porter has 'the top three buttons of his uniform unfastened'; and the pair of slippers that Mrs Fiedke buys for her nephew are size nine (three threes). Sevens abound: the action takes place in July, the seventh month; at the office Lise has seven colleagues over her, another seven beneath her (with her female colleagues in mainly subordinate roles); Bill tells her his diet is Regime 7, and arranges to meet her at seven o'clock; there are six men in Carlo's garage, which with Lise makes a group of seven; a family of seven (two parents and five children) are mentioned casually; the passengers leave from Gate 14 (two sevens); and among the times specifically referred to, with slightly excessive precision, are 2.12 and 4.10 (both adding up to fourteen). The narrative itself is divided into seven chapters.

The statement in a novel that the time is 2.12 may strike us as having an odd, unfamiliar, slightly obsessive flavour: railway timetables find it necessary to refer to the clock with such precision, but novelists don't usually feel the need to do so. One effect of such touches is parodic, as if in sardonic or playful imitation of the conventions of formal realism that habitually call for the retailing of precise but unimportant details. More importantly, the numerological patterns, like the other repetitions and symmetries, and like the garments referred to in the opening pages with their closed shapes and rigid parallel lines, may suggest something of the tormented inner life of the psychotic. (Pattern, including mathematical patterns, is used in a somewhat similar way by Samuel Beckett, for instance in his novel *Watt*; and the black comedy of *The Driver's Seat* has at moments a distinctly Beckettian manner.)

But the world of mathematics also reassures us that we do not inhabit a universe that is wholly random and unpredictable, and it can be argued that the kind of patterning we have been noting endows the world of the novel with meaning and hence works in the opposite direction from what seems to be the merely fortuitous and meaningless, just as Lise's sense of mission shapes all the chance happenings of the action. That which most obviously endows the trivial with significance and conceives of life as moving towards a definite goal is religious faith, which regards even the fall of a sparrow as part of an all-embracing eternal pattern. In this way the formal qualities of the novel work in the opposite direction from the physical and social world it creates, and a sense of the transcendental seems to underlie the bleak, indifferent world of contingency that Lise inhabits. The reader of this text will discern further elements of patterning that have not been identified here: consider, for example, the use of coincidence (for example, the two meetings with the elderly English aristocrat) and parallel episodes (Lise's visits to department stores in two countries, her meeting with elderly foreign ladies before and after her journey, the two cars she drives, etc.).

As in some of the novels already discussed, there is in *The Driver's Seat* some implicit wordplay related to plots and plotting. The plot of the novel corresponds to the plot of her own life and death that Lise has written: to be in the driver's seat is to be, whether literally or metaphorically, in charge. But the ending of the novel shows that Lise's belief in her capacity for self-determination is no more than a delusion: it is after all God, not man or woman, who writes the plots of our lives. When she instructs her murderer to tie her ankles he refuses and 'plunges into her, with the knife held high'. 'Plunges', used punningly here, can easily be misread as the act of stabbing her, but actually refers to the sexual act, and it is another two lines before 'the knife', still 'held high', 'descends to her throat'. Ultimately she has been unable, as we all are, to control her own destiny, to write the script of her own life and death.

With Lise dead, the novel's final sentence shows the murderer looking forward, beyond the limits of the text, to his own arrest and interrogation, where the police will wear uniforms and adopt official, depersonalised stances 'devised to protect them from the indecent exposure of fear and pity, pity and fear'. This is one of the few passages in the book (striking because so few) in which the style becomes suddenly and momentarily lyrical or rhetorical. The last six words, a final symmetrical pattern, recall the discussion of tragedy in Aristotle's *Poetics* and remind us that, for all its contemporary setting, this work has a classic concentration and singleness of purpose as well as largely confining itself to the 24 hours assumed to be referred to by Aristotle as the duration of the tragic action. There have not been many previous references to human emotions: indeed, the narrative has shown them mainly in a debased form (love being represented by the lust of Bill and Carlo, family affection by Lise's pathetic purchase of gifts for non-existent relatives, social and political concern by the street riot), but the novel closes by asserting the importance of what makes us human.

It is easy to say what *The Driver's Seat* does not offer. The development of character and relationships, the exercise of choice and the making of decisions – these concerns of mainstream fiction are largely absent. Lise is shown only from the outside – at one point the narrator demands 'Who knows her thoughts?

Who can tell?' – but in any case she seems dominated, almost programmed, by an obsession that directs her, like a driver, along a determined route. Trapped within the private experience of a psychotic, she is quite different from Muriel Spark's earlier heroines and can make no assertion of her individual freedom as Annabel does in *The Public Image*. But the parabolic quality of the novel discourages us from dismissing her as an eccentric case, and the hints of public events (the student demonstration, the coup in the Arab's country) imply a world of widespread disorder and violence in which the central drama of Lise's death takes its place.

Reviewing *The Driver's Seat* when it appeared in 1970, Frank Kermode commented that there is in it 'nothing to remind one of the writer's religious plots',[57] but what has already been said about the ending of the novel may lead one to differ with this judgement. The title is, ultimately, ironical, for it can be only by means of an illusion that we can suppose ourselves to be in the driver's seat of our lives. Certainly the religious element is much less explicit than in some of the earlier novels, but it seems more obviously present, and important, than in *The Public Image*. It is possible that Muriel Spark learned something from one of the best-known novels of the leading contemporary religious novelist in English. Graham Greene's *Brighton Rock* (1938) has as its opening sentence 'Hale knew, before he had been in Brighton three hours, that they meant to murder him', and later Hale, employed by a newspaper in a publicity campaign, is obliged, even as he seeks to escape his killers, to leave a trail by which they can pursue him. At the same time Pinkie, the leader of the criminal gang, lays a trail of his own: 'It was as if he were talking in the witness box, giving the evidence he was meant to give'. Greene, however, writes a novel that is much closer to traditional narrative conventions and has an interest in character that has no counterpart in *The Driver's Seat*. What Muriel Spark's novel has to offer is something more limited but extremely powerful, in the manner of parable: intellectually exciting, with the fascination that belongs to a subtle and intricate game, and with constant stylistic surprises and gratifications, it also has a fundamental seriousness that coexists with the absurdism or black comedy of its surface. I have known readers who have found it distasteful, even repellent, but it seems possible that they have brought to it expectations derived from other kinds of fiction rather than allowing it to create the rules that govern its own nature, as any truly original work of art can do.

For Alan Bold, *The Driver's Seat* and the two novels that followed it, *Not to Disturb* and *The Hothouse by the East River*, constitute 'a macabre poetic trilogy';[58] but a different kind of grouping is possible, and there is a sense in which *Not to Disturb* combines and refines the preoccupations of its two predecessors, *The Public Image* and *The Driver's Seat*. From the former comes its sardonic exposure of the power of the mass media in the contemporary world: the main characters are motivated by the wish to get their hands on the vast fortunes to be made by supplying sensational and scandalous material to the mass-circulation magazines and the film industry. Its relationship to *The Driver's Seat* is more subtle: like that novel it is end-directed, but the situation is now turned inside out. Whereas the reader followed the inevitable progress of Lise from her attempt on the first page to buy a dress that will show stains to her death on the last page, in *Not to Disturb* the victims are insubstantial figures and the violence takes place behind locked doors (or, in the terms of stage tragedy, off-stage). It is as if a piece of tapestry were seen from the wrong side: the reader is privy not to the 'events' themselves but to their making and their exploitation, the spinning of a plot that is acted out by largely invisible performers.

Compared with *The Driver's Seat*, *Not to Disturb* has an even more intense concentration: Lise crosses Europe and moves through a series of locations towards her doom, but the entire action of the later novel takes place in the castle and its grounds and occupies no more than a few hours, from one evening to the early morning of the next day. This conformity to the Aristotelian tragic formula is no doubt, like much else, parodic, for this is a very literary book in the sense that it invokes genres, conventions and styles in order to expose their artifice. The chief character, Lister (whose name bears a curious resemblance to that of Lise), is incorrigibly bookish: his first speech contains a quotation from Webster's *The Duchess of Malfi*, and subsequent speeches constitute a Golden Treasury of English verse. We also have a madman in the attic, a dark and stormy night in which people beat on the doors and beg for admission, a dead baron in the locked library, and other reminders of the artifice on which so many literary works depend. In his brilliant and penetrating

discussion of this novel Peter Kemp has explored its use of motifs
from the Gothic horror tale and from Jacobean tragedy.

The plot-maker is Lister, leader of and spokesman for the
servants who are, in this novel, not minor characters in supporting
roles but foregrounded so that the action is seen from their point
of view. At the beginning of the final chapter (the five chapters
corresponding to the five acts of a classic tragedy) Lister reminds
his fellow servants that '"when dealing with the rich, the
journalists are mainly interested in backstairs chatter. The
popular glossy magazines have replaced the servants' hall in
modern society. Our position of privilege is unparalleled in
history"' (p. 137; references are to the 1971 edition). Anticipating
or prophesying the tragic outcome, Lister masterminds a complex
programme of contractual commitments whereby he and other
servants will be able to profit from the double murder and suicide
that have not yet taken place but are seen as inevitable. The
Baron, the Baroness, and her lover (another literary convention,
the 'eternal triangle') will all die in the locked room to which
they have withdrawn. Meanwhile their employees await the
outcome, journalists and film-makers stand by, and last-minute
arrangements are made for profiting by the deaths (Lister
remarks complacently that he made his contracts '"with *Stern*
and *Paris-Match* over a month ago"' (p. 8)).

When Lister's plot is threatened by contingency, he quickly
steps in to safeguard the inevitability of what he has foreseen. It
emerges that the lunatic in the attic is the Baron's heir, so he is
quickly married off to one of the servants. A couple of minor
characters turn up at the castle – 'life', untidy as ever, intruding
on the mechanical efficiency of 'plot' – but Lister coolly remarks
that '"They don't come into the story"' (p. 51), and they are
later dispatched by a convenient bolt of lightning; even their
death, 'instantly without pain', as Ruth Whittaker points out,
does not humanise them.

The setting is Switzerland, but, like the characters in Beckett's
Waiting for Godot and the shadowy figures in Eliot's *The Waste
Land*, the servants, if their names are anything to go by, are an
international or perhaps a stateless crowd: Lister seems to be
English, but his colleagues include Pablo the handyman, Heloise
the maid, Clovis the chef, Hadrian his assistant, and Sister
Barton the nurse. Theo and Clara, who live in the lodge, have
previously worked in Madrid, and one has a sense of an itinerant,

rootless workforce prepared to go wherever the pickings are good and without affection or allegiance for any spot on earth – a backstairs equivalent of the cosmopolitan world of the film industry depicted in *The Public Image*.

Any sense of traditional loyalties, of being (in Yeats's phrase) 'rooted in one dear perpetual place', is also lacking where we might most expect to find it: in the house and its aristocratic owners. The Baron and Baroness are once or twice referred to as Cecil and Cathy Klopstock, names that sound not only unbaronial but unSwiss, inviting speculation as to their origins and the source of their fortune, while the house itself, for all its Gothic atmosphere, is no ancestral pile but a mere eleven years old and an assemblage of spare parts ripped and raided from different parts of Europe: an Adam mantelpiece has 'come through the Swiss customs' (p. 42), and Lister comments on the origin of the parquet flooring, which

'. . . once belonged to a foreign king. He had to flee his throne. He took the parquet of his palace with him, also the door-knobs. Royalty always do, when they have to leave. They take everything, like stage-companies who need their props. With royalty, of course, it all is largely a matter of stage production. And lighting. Royalty are very careful about their setting and their lighting. As is the Pope. . . .' (p. 45)

Such a passage is characteristic of the tone and method of the whole book in its combination of a surrealistically comic or absurd surface (the grotesque image of the crowned heads of Europe fleeing their thrones with parquet and door-knobs in their luggage) and the implication of violent and tragic events, revolution and exile.

The absurdism is an important element and helps to make *Not to Disturb* a very entertaining book in spite of the blackness of its theme. From the opening lines the dialogue – and a very large proportion of the book is to consist of dialogue – is stylised and polished in the manner of Ivy Compton-Burnett; but unlike the novels of that author it contains an engaging zaniness. In the following exchange Lister is trying to persuade his aunt Eleanor, who is actually younger than him, to agree to marry him:

He says, rising to approach her, 'Aunt to me though you
are, would you marry me outside the Book of Common
Prayer?'

She says, 'I have my scruples and I'm proud of them.'

He says, 'In France an aunt may marry a nephew.'

'No, Lister, I stand by the Table of Kindred and Affinity.
I don't want to get heated at this moment, on this night,
Lister. You're starting me off. The press and the police are
coming, and there are only sixty-four shopping days to
Christmas.' (p. 48)

At such moments Ronald Firbank and Max Beerbohm seem
more potent influences than Jacobean tragedy or Gothic fiction.
But, as Peter Kemp has argued, with its emphasis on dialogue,
its respect for the unities, its 'resounding curtain-lines', its
restriction to external presentation of characters ('only their
actions and their speech recorded'), and its resolute march
towards a foreseen tragic outcome, the novel has a strongly
dramatic quality and is 'close to a transcript of something
occurring on a stage'.[59]

As in *The Driver's Seat* the narrative is in the present tense, as
if the action were unfolding before the reader's eyes and without
the intervention of a narrator enjoying privileged status and
superior knowledge. Paradoxically, although at any given point
the future has not yet happened, it is known and referred to in
a way that even retrospective narrative normally eschews. The
result is an indifference to suspense, that usual preoccupation of
the storyteller's art: the three who are to die are merely acting
out a scenario, performing a script, as if they were characters in
a play or film, in order to justify the lucrative 'scandal exclusives'
(p. 144) that the servants have sold to the media.

The grammatical counterpart of the paradox is the wobbly
nature of the tenses in certain passages:

'The poor late Baron,' says Heloise.

'Precisely,' says Lister. 'He'll be turning up soon. In the
Buick, I should imagine.' (p. 7)

The Baron is both dead, or as good as dead, and yet to arrive
for the denouement; but since, as Muriel Spark puts it in her
essay on Proust, 'the whole of eternity is present "now"', time

and tense are in any case artificial human constructs. Another passage executes a more complicated movement between tenses:

'Suppose the Baron wants his dinner?'
'Of course he expected his dinner,' Lister says. 'But as things turned out he didn't live to eat it. He'll be arriving soon.'
'There might be an unexpected turn of events,' says Eleanor.
'There was sure to be something unexpected,' says Lister. 'But what's done is about to be done and the future has come to pass. My memoirs up to the funeral are as a matter of fact more or less complete. At all events it's out of our hands. . . .' (pp. 11–12)

Here we seem not far from *Alice in Wonderland*, where the Queen of Hearts wants to pass sentence and then hear the verdict: Lister has written an account of an event and now awaits its happening. Implicit in this, of course, is (again, as in *The Public Image*) a sardonic commentary on the fictive nature of 'news' as reported by the popular press and other media. It also recalls Muriel Spark's longstanding and more broadly based interest in the relationship between 'events' and the literary or fictional artefacts that purport to represent them. Lister is one of her makers of fiction, and like some earlier incarnations of this type his plot comes 'true'. (Ruth Whittaker shrewdly notes that 'The novel is filled with jargon relating to the making of fictions, the welding together of events'.[60])

At one point the time-bound world and its literary counterpart, tense-restricted narrative, are explicitly rejected:

'I'll see the Baron in the morning. I have to talk to him,' says Mr McGuire.
'Too late,' says Lister. 'The Baron is no more.'
'I can hear his voice. What d'you mean?'
'Let us not strain after vulgar chronology.' says Lister. . . . (p. 66)

Again Ruth Whittaker provides an apt comment: ' "Vulgar chronology" is Mrs Spark's view of chronological time, and for her the act of writing is in itself what she has called "an attempt to redeem the time"' (the phrase occurs in her interview with Frank Kermode).[61]

Alan Bold plausibly sees *Not to Disturb* as an attempt to ridicule determinism: something as preposterous and repellent as this is where such a doctrine leads us, and 'a world devoid of free will would be as soul-destroying as Lister's scenario'.[62] Ruth Whittaker's view of it as 'a sardonic admission that for most people worldly plots do indeed take precedence over God's plots'[63] is not inconsistent with this. It is also perhaps a warning of what we can expect if we believe that life resembles art: Lister's preoccupation with a perfectly mechanical plot and with form are ultimately absurd, as one of his aphorisms makes clear: 'To put it squarely, as I say in my memoir, the eternal triangle has come full circle' (p. 39). His geometrical clichés, like his near-namesake Lise's rigidly geometrical furnishings, imply a rejection of life.

Alan Bold characterises *The Hothouse by the East River* as a 'fantasy' and, as already noted, groups it with its two immediate predecessors, describing it as the last of 'three experimental novels'.[64] 'Fantasy' and 'experimental', however, are terms that can be applied more widely to Muriel Spark's fiction, and there are respects in which *Hothouse* differs from *The Driver's Seat* and *Not to Disturb*. Whereas these two novels march relentlessly towards inevitable deaths, in *Hothouse* the deaths have taken place long before the 'action' of the novel begins: its characters are not so much unable to avoid their own imminent deaths as unwilling to accept the fact of their deaths that took place long ago. This is, in other words, an inversion of the earlier theme, and inversion is one of the recurring motifs of the work. A woman's shadow falls the wrong way, producing darkness where there ought to be light; a performance of the children's play *Peter Pan* is staged by a geriatric cast; and the 'hothouse' of an overheated apartment in a highrise block in winter is actually Purgatory.

Paul and Elsa Hazlett have in fact been killed in England in 1944 as a result of a direct hit by a German bomb on the train in which they were sitting. They had planned to emigrate once the war was over and to make a new life in New York, and the story presents the life of affluence that might have been theirs if they had survived. Like the protagonist of William Golding's

Pincher Martin (1956) they refuse to accept their own deaths; whereas Golding's theological drama is acted out on an isolated rock in mid-Atlantic, however, Muriel Spark makes a complete crossing of the Atlantic and draws on her own experience of living in New York to portray the unreality, even the absurdity, of modern urban civilisation. There are familiar elements of satire and parody – for example, of the spy thriller and the ghost story as well as of J. M. Barrie's *Peter Pan*, staged by the Hazletts' son Pierre, the son they never had and hence, like Barrie's hero, the boy who never grew up. Again, the parodic method involves inversion, for this is a ghost story in which the dead are haunted by the living:

> How long, cries Paul in his heart, will these people, this city, haunt me? 'Elsa,' he says, 'be yourself. Just be yourself, I ask you.' (1973 edition, p. 104)

But to be herself – a dead woman – is precisely what Elsa, until the last words of the novel, is unable or unwilling to do.

At the end, the Hazletts watch their apartment block being demolished: 'The morning breeze from the East River is already spreading the dust' (p. 167), and since this is a text in which tiny, apparently trivial details carry a substantial burden of meaning we may think of the dust as that associated with mortality and the grave as well as with a demolition site. ' "Now we can have some peace," says Elsa' also suggests the peace in which, according to graveyard inscriptions, the dead rest. Like *The Driver's Seat*, then, *Hothouse* seems to end with inevitable deaths; but it is, more exactly, the acceptance of death that forms the conclusion, and the deaths themselves have occurred long ago. As Peter Kemp says in his excellent analysis of this novel, it is 'a sinister book . . . in which everything occurs the wrong way round'[65] (Kemp rightly sees the inverted shadow both as a central image and as related to the parodic use of *Peter Pan*, a fantasy in which a detachable shadow plays a part). It might be argued that this is not the first novel in which everything happens 'the wrong way round'; in *The Driver's Seat* the murderer–victim roles are reversed, in *Not to Disturb* media exploitation precedes instead of following a sensational event. But Kemp is right to insist that this is a novel more consistently dominated by absurdity, even insanity.

Like these other novels, *Hothouse* is narrated in a present tense
that seems to remove the events from the dimension of time.
There are other elements that are by now familiar features of
Muriel Spark's work. It is a fiction that is, among other things,
about fiction, partly because its main characters are, like so many
other characters in other novels, fiction-makers, inventing a life
that has never been lived, but also through its intimate and
creative relationship with other forms of fiction. To quote Peter
Kemp again, 'To compose this book, several types of literature
have been torn apart and their components, clichés and conventions of the mode, cunningly reworked into a collage that is
tortuously didactic, calculatedly absurd'. Kemp sees the whole
work, indeed, as a sustained enactment of the central principle
of inversion, and hence 'an ultimate in anti-novels since it bears
that relationship to traditional fiction that a negative does to a
positive'. His conclusion is that, while not the most successful
of Muriel Spark's books, it is 'extremely comprehensive, a
compressed and involuted anthology of all her most characteristic
techniques and concerns'.[66]

Even by Muriel Spark's usual standards it is a subtle and
allusive novel, and some readers have found it not only difficult,
but distasteful. Even the author's characteristic wit and humour
have here become 'sick', as in the scene in which a woman who
breeds silkworms by keeping their eggs warm in her bosom is
seen to have her flesh crawling with the newly hatched creatures –
a nightmarish, surrealistic depiction of a 'living' woman as a
rotting corpse. A biographical interpretation might suggest that
it expresses some of the feelings that led the author to terminate
her period of residence in New York and return to Europe. But
it is a serious and passionate story, and its central affirmation,
enunciated in a brief burst of narratorial authority and in
resonant, biblical tones, rejects the perverse, the distorted, the
inverted and the self-deceiving out of hand: 'One should live
first, then die, not die then live; everything to its own time'
(p. 142). The novel has no truck with Barrie's sentimental
conclusion in *Peter Pan* that 'to die will be an awfully big
adventure': like William Golding, its author exposes the conceit
and the mad folly of clinging to the shadows of earthly life, and
as Elsa moves at the end towards the car that will carry her
away towards an accepted state of death she 'trails her faithful
and lithe cloud of unknowing across the pavement'. The final

double allusion is to the fourteenth-century English mystical work *The Cloud of Unknowing* and also to the 'cloud' in the final sentence of *The Ballad of Peckham Rye*. If the latter was indeed a conscious reference, it must have occurred to Muriel Spark that her fiction had travelled a very long way in the thirteen years that separate that genial, relaxed and very English book from the febrile and anguished intensity of her American novel.

The Abbess of Crewe sits somewhat oddly and unexpectedly between the severe novels that immediately precede and follow it, respectively *The Hothouse by the East River* and *The Takeover*, and both the label on the paperback edition ('A wicked satire on Watergate') and the title of the film version (*Nasty Habits*) suggest a mode and mood alien to the general tenor of Muriel Spark's fiction in the 1970s. The book is very short, even by this author's usual standard, and it would be tempting to dismiss it as a joke or a *jeu d'esprit*, and to relegate it to the margin of her output, if it did not contain some familiar elements among much that is less familiar.

Satire is usually topical, and *The Abbess of Crewe* has an obvious topicality: the year of its publication (1974) is also the year in which, following the Watergate scandal, Richard Nixon resigned, in mid-term, from the Presidency of the United States, and there are some parallels with notable features of the Nixon administration (Sister Gertrude, the wayward missionary constantly jetting from one part of the globe to another, is Henry Kissinger in drag) and of the Watergate investigation (the Abbess has Nixon's habit of taping private conversations; she then, when necessary, doctors the tapes). But we should perhaps not be in too much of a hurry to accept the description of this novel or novella as a satire: all we know of Muriel Spark to this date suggests that, although she has many of the qualifications for a satirist (the wit and inventiveness as well as the critical, questioning view of people and society), she lacks an essential attribute of the true satirist, who, moved to anger or indignation or contempt by the world's folly and wickedness, wants to expose things as they are in order to change them, to make the world a better place. This is surely not the kind of writer we have encountered in the dozen novels that precede this one. Fully aware of human folly and sin, Muriel Spark accepts them as part of the order of things. She knows that all is not for the best in the best of all possible worlds, but she does not share the reformer's zeal since she has no confidence that tinkering with, or even overthrowing, regimes or institutions will make much contribution to solving 'the only problem', that of evil and suffering. Most satire is social and political, but Muriel Spark's theological preoccupations exist on a different plane, and Ruth Whittaker is surely right when she says that this novel 'lacks the didactic weight of satire'.[67]

At the same time the Abbess Alexandra is, beneath her habit, a recognisable Spark heroine – closest, perhaps, to Jean Brodie, whose outrageous vivacity and brio she shares (though not her pathos, since the longer perspective of time in the earlier novel is missing from the more confined world – temporally as well as spatially – of the Abbey of Crewe). Like so many of the heroines, Alexandra is a plot-maker, and there is a passage at the end of Chapter 4 that suggests she is also an artist:

> 'Oh, have I got to do it again?' Winifrede says in her little wailing voice.
> 'Possibly,' says the Abbess. 'Meantime go and rest before Compline. After Compline we shall all meet here for refreshments and some entertaining scenarios. Think up your best scenarios, Sisters.'
> 'What are scenarios?' says Winifrede.
> 'They are an art-form,' says the Abbess of Crewe, 'based on facts. A good scenario is a garble. A bad one is a bungle. They need not be plausible, only hypnotic, like all good art.'

With a familiar stylistic gambit, the writer places the last four words of the sentence and the chapter so that the field of reference suddenly becomes both wider and more serious. 'Scenario', originally a term of dramatic and cinematic art, has been appropriated for more worldly contexts, and here refers to the fictions imposed by politicians on the public: political statements are 'an art-form . . . based on facts' but, like novels, under no obligation to adhere to them. A successful politician like Alexandra is, it is implied, a fiction-maker: her inventions, like those of the novelist, 'need not be plausible, only hypnotic, like all good art'.

At the end of the novel Alexandra, having manipulated the media, made a successful appearance on television, and 'given the orders for the selection and orchestration of the transcripts of her tape-recordings', is serenely on her way to Rome to appear before a 'Congregational Committee of Investigation'. There seems no reason to suppose that she will not survive its questioning with her self-confidence and her reputation unimpaired, and it is clear that her career is not parallel to that of Nixon. Despite occasional touches – the Congregational Committee is only a few letters removed from the Congressional Committee, and at one point, referring to the state of affairs in the Abbey, she says that 'Such a scandal could never arise in the United States of America' – the political satire is in fact fairly perfunctory. Although Ruth Whittaker claims that '*The Abbess of Crewe* satirises power and its corrupting influence, the reforms of the Catholic Church [especially in the figure of the liberal nun Felicity], and the farcical nature of world politics', she also concedes that at the end of the novel Alexandra is 'given an elaborate and sustaining endorsement, which implicitly grants approval to her activities throughout the novel'.[68] This can only mean that the Alexandra/Nixon parallel has been abandoned; and indeed there has from the start been little sign that Alexandra's zestful manipulation of people and events is intended to be other than entertaining in its panache and stylishness. If the book begins as satire it soon turns into a delightful game.

This makes it very hard to accept Alan Bold's characterising of Alexandra as 'arrogant', 'self-centred to the point of self-destruction', 'gifted yet ultimately idiotic in her abuse of personal power', and 'truly corrupt in her conviction that foul means justify a selfish end'.[69] Such a character would be an interesting one, but it seems to bear little resemblance to Alexandra, and Bold's severe judgement makes a little surprising his admission that the author is on Alexandra's side: 'If Spark sympathises with her it is because Alexandra has the egotism of the artist, adamant that she has a right to compel others into acting out the drama of her destiny'. More persuasive to my mind is John Updike's observation in his *New Yorker* review of the novel that Muriel Spark evidently loves Alexandra 'as she hasn't loved a character in a decade'. A little more than a decade takes us back to *The Ballad of Peckham Rye* and *The Prime of Miss Jean Brodie*, and *The Abbess of Crewe* seems to be a throwback to these earlier books – and not necessarily the worse for that. When Alexandra tells Gertrude near the end of the book that she herself has

'become an object of art, the end of which is to give pleasure',
Muriel Spark may be scoring a palpable hit at politicians who
project a public image that belongs to the art of fiction (Alexandra
has referred in the same speech to 'many film and stage offers');
she is also surely disclaiming the satirist's moral purpose.

This short novel returns to one of Muriel Spark's favourite
themes: the relationship between reality and art; and when
Alexandra says that she has 'become an object of art' we may
express this by saying that the Abbess of Crewe has become *The
Abbess of Crewe*, just as Alexandra's plots are also the novel's
plot. In a sense, then, Alexandra has 'written' the novel. It is
not difficult to make harsh judgements about her unscrupulousness and her worldliness, but moral activity of this kind is not
likely to be an element in the experience of reading this novel,
which does nothing to encourage judgements on Alexandra. And
since judgement, on the part of writer and reader, is essential to
satire, it looks as though this is almost the last word that should
properly be applied to *The Abbess of Crewe*.

In her bravura, her unscrupulousness and her moral nullity,
Maggie, the heroine (or anti-heroine) of *The Takeover* has much
in common with Alexandra. Having depicted – with relish and
without explicit censure – corruption and intrigue in an English
religious house, Muriel Spark in her next two novels depicts
corruption and intrigue in Italy. That country had by now
become her own and had already been the setting for *The Public
Image* and *The Driver's Seat*. It is very much a contemporary Italy,
and the time scheme in *The Takeover* is highly specific. The story
opens in 1973: 'The morning news had announced the death of
Noël Coward, calling it "the passing of an era"' (p. 12: references
to the 1976 edition), and the journalistic cliché has, for once, to
be taken seriously, for the narrative, which extends to 1975,
depicts a world that seems to be on the brink of economic and
moral collapse. As Ruth Whittaker says in her penetrating
analysis of this novel, whereas most of Muriel Spark's plots 'have
a hermetic quality, dealing with enclosed communities or groups
of people bound together by common circumstances', *The Takeover*
is an exception in that 'its characters are strongly under pressure
from the economic and political changes in the wider world'.[70]
Halfway through the book the narrator observes of a group of
characters that 'it was not in their minds at the time that this

last quarter of the year they had entered, that of 1973, was in fact the beginning of something new in their world; a change in the meaning of property and money' (pp. 126–7). *The Takeover* is a novel about property and money and their effects on human lives and relationships: apparently lacking the theological dimension that we have come to expect in a novel by Muriel Spark, it in fact depicts the emptiness of the lives of those for whom God does not exist.

That label applies to most of the characters, but not quite all, for Pauline Thin (her name links her with St Paul, from whom she quotes) is a Catholic and, in her independence and her unconventionally, has something in common with such earlier figures as Caroline Rose in *The Comforters*. Early Christianity took over various pagan cults (one of the several meanings hinted at by the novel's title), and the setting for a large part of the action is Nemi, ancient site of the worship of the pagan goddess Diana. Hubert Mallindaine, homosexual and trickster, claims to be descended from Diana: this time the name has a more complex significance, since he claims that the latter part of his surname (-daine) is a form of 'Diana', but the implications of 'Mallin' (malign) seem more accurate. Hubert establishes a lucrative cult with himself as high priest; as often, Muriel Spark is implicitly contrasting true belief with credulity and fraudulence (cf. the use of spiritualism in *The Bachelors*). Hubert insists that Nemi is his 'ancestral home' (p. 89); the sordid fact is that he is occupying a house that belongs to Maggie and refuses to move out even though she wishes to be rid of him – another significance of the title.

Religion, mythology and magic are important in this novel, and a passage near the beginning refers to Sir James Frazer's 'massive testament to comparative religion', *The Golden Bough*, published in twelve volumes between 1890 and 1915. As these dates suggest, this work of late-Victorian scholarship might also be said to have marked 'the end of an era'. But the allusion shifts, within a single sentence, from a scholarly note to a revelation of Hubert's obsession, shared by so many characters in the book, with money:

> The very panorama of Nemi, the lake, the most lush vegetation on earth, the scene which had stirred the imagin- ation of Sir James Frazer at the beginning of . . . *The Golden*

Bough, all this magical influence and scene which had never before failed in their effects, all the years he had known the place and in the months he had lived there, suddenly was too expensive. I can't afford the view, thought Hubert and turned back into the room. (pp. 10–11)

Later (pp. 56–8) Muriel Spark quotes at length from Frazer's book, and also adapts for her own purposes his phrase 'the scene of the tragedy':

This tragedy was only so in the classical and dramatic sense; its participants were in perfect collusion. In the historic sense it was a pathetic and greedy affair. The recurrent performance of the tragedy began before the dates of knowledge, in mythology, but repeating itself tenaciously well into known history. (pp. 55–6)

'A pathetic and greedy affair' might plausibly be taken as a comment on the lives of the main characters and on their actions and motivations.

In the world of *The Takeover*, religion, mythology, magic and mystery have all become debased and flourish only as fraud and superstition. The narrator, usually noncommittal, makes this quite clear with respect to Hubert:

Hubert descended, then, from the Emperor [Caligula], the goddess [Diana], and from her woodland priest; in reality this was nothing more than his synthesis of a persistent, yet far more vague, little story fostered by a couple of dotty aunts enamoured of the author-image of Sir James Frazer and misled by one of those quack genealogists who flourished in late Victorian times and around the turn of the century, and who still, when they take up the trade, never fail to flourish. (p. 58)

By the end of the same chapter the narratorial impartiality or indifference has returned:

Again, standing one winter day alone among the bare soughing branches of those thick woodlands, looking down at the furrowed rectangle where the goddess was worshipped long ago, [Hubert] shouted aloud with great enthusiasm, 'It's

mine! I am the king of Nemi! It is my divine right! I am
Hubert Mallindaine the descendant of the Emperor of Rome
and the Benevolent-Malign Diana of the Woods. . . .' And
whether he was sincere or not; or whether, indeed, he was or
was not connected so far back as the divinity-crazed Caligula –
and if he was descended from any gods of mythology, purely
on statistical grounds who is not? – at any rate, these words
were what Hubert cried. (p. 60)

The reference to the late Roman emperor Caligula gives a
historical as well as a mythological perspective to this story of
modern Italy, linking the corruption, decadence and violence of
modern society with similar conditions two thousand years
earlier.

Hubert's cult attracts a good number of followers, recruited
from the drifting, well-to-do, cosmopolitan crowd who were eager
to expend their credulity in the Seventies on any quasi-religious
movement that also offered opportunities for indulgence in drugs
and sex. Even the normally shrewd Maggie is infected with
superstitious fear:

> 'Do you believe in the evil eye?' said Maggie still speaking
> very low.
> 'Well, no,' said Mary whispering back in concert, 'I believe
> I don't.' She bent closer to Maggie.
> 'It's possible,' Maggie breathed, 'that if there is such a
> thing, Hubert has the evil eye. . . . (p. 53)

But Maggie's real god is money: we are repeatedly reminded
that she is 'spectacularly rich' (p. 76) and has 'enormous wealth'
(p. 87). She belongs to an international set of very rich people
whom jet travel has enabled to treat the entire globe as if it
consisted of a single vast estate designed for their pleasure,
'people who at that time woke and took breakfast, as it might
be, in Monte Carlo, flew to Venice for a special dinner, Milan
next evening for the opera, Portugal for a game of golf and
Gstaad for the week-end' (p. 96).

For Maggie and her like, religious faith (and she lives in Italy,
the centre of the Roman Catholic world) has dwindled into
superstition and credulity, the Trinity trivialised into the three
houses at Nemi which she owns and the three husbands she

successively acquired (the allusions to the magic properties of
the number three recall *The Driver's Seat*). Similarly, the chastity
associated with the goddess Diana has been corrupted into a
sexual game: the servant Lauro, ambitious and predatory like
the servants in *Not to Disturb*, sleeps indifferently, in both senses
of the word, with Maggie, her daughter-in-law and her husband.
We are reminded that even in the ancient world Diana was
exploited, for the New Testament tells how the Ephesian sil-
versmiths, their livelihood threatened by the spread of Christianity, launched a publicity campaign to boost sales of their images
of the goddess (see *Acts*, chapter 28).

In the course of the rich and complex comic plot, Maggie is
deprived of her wealth as a result of putting her faith in swindlers.
The religion of wealth turns out to be as baseless as the house
she has built – it was three years in the building – which is the
subject of the quarrel between her and Hubert: it turns out that
she has been cheated from the outset and does not even own the
land on which it has been constructed. Hubert's fake religion is
matched by the fake antiques and paintings that he substitutes
for the genuine ones in Maggie's house; by a nice touch one of
the paintings she has bought as genuine turns out to be a fake,
and 'fake' is indeed a keyword in this novel. Fake artefacts, fake
legal documents, fake mythology and genealogy, fake etymology
of a name, a fake religious cult: deceptions and their exposure
operate on many levels and symbolise the hollowness of the lives
led by the rich cosmopolitans. What had been shown in *The
Public Image* in relation to a particular profession, the film
industry, is here shown to be true of a whole section of society.

Ruth Whittaker's summarising comment on *The Takeover* and
the novel that immediately follows it brings out the positive
implications of what may otherwise seem to be a negative, even
cynical or despairing, view of the modern world:

In a world without religious faith as a source of security,
material goods may seem a measure of stability, but Mrs
Spark sabotages that belief. Faith in the material is shown to
be misplaced and possession itself a farce; territorial claims,
whether related to real estate or sexual monopoly, are dramatically undermined. Both these novels are set in contemporary
Italy, where the impression is given that the twentieth-century

decline and fall is speeded-up and intensified; this acts as emblematic of Mrs Spark's view of the world at large.[71]

As already noted, though, it is not merely contemporary Italy but the Western world at a particular point in its recent history that is portrayed. Opening in 1973, the novel has by its midpoint reached the following year, and the private enterprises of its self-seeking characters are placed in the context of world events: 'A little over a year had passed since the Middle East war of 1973, and Hubert was fairly flourishing on the ensuing crisis. He had founded a church. . .' (p. 139). Hubert's pseudo-religion is thus directly connected with the economic crisis: the adherents of the new faith are those whose affluent lifestyles are threatened by political and economic developments. By the following chapter it is 1975 (p. 151) and we are very close to, perhaps coincident with, the date of composition.

When Maggie finds herself unable to expel an intruder who is bathing off what she regards as her private beach, she is described as 'aware of her impotence in territorial rights' (p. 114), and when Lauro visits a cemetery he views the 'small oblong territorial properties of the family dead' (p. 80). The earlier of these two novels thus contains hints of the title of its successor and both novels draw on the primary, legalistic meanings of their titles, both of which relate to the ownership of property or land, as well as on secondary, wider meanings. The two novels have much in common, including the fact that they are somewhat longer than Muriel Spark's average.

The setting of *Territorial Rights* is Venice, a city on which a number of foreigners converge. Arnold Leaver, headmaster of an English private school, comes to Venice with his mistress, Mary Tiller, leaving his wife Anthea in Birmingham. Anthea is a bored suburban housewife who finds solace in reading a library book, passages from which are quoted at intervals: it is in a vein of domestic realism that is emphatically not Muriel Spark's own novelistic manner, and its banalities are apparently offered as 'significant', but actually constitute a parody of a familiar kind of contemporary fiction. Arnold's son, Robert Leaver, also turns up in Venice from Paris, where he has been a male prostitute and the protégé of a wealthy American homosexual and art collector, Mark Curran. (The reference to works of art in association with wealth recalls Maggie's collection in *The Take-over.*) Robert Leaver later becomes a blackmailer, a bank robber and an international terrorist.

The Pensione Sofia, where the story opens, is kept by two sisters who have both formerly been in love with Pancev, a Bulgarian politician killed in Venice at the end of the war. Lina, Pancev's daughter, has fled to the West and has come to Venice to find out what she can about her father's death; it turns out that his corpse was cut in half by a local butcher and the two halves buried in different areas of the garden of the Pensione Sofia – areas over which the two sisters have respectively established 'territorial rights', thus claiming an equal share of the man they have both loved. One of the most bizarre scenes in a novel which has no shortage of the extravagant, the absurd and the vicious occurs when Lina is prevailed upon to dance on the spot where her father lies buried, without realising what she is doing.

As this brief listing of the main characters makes clear, this is, like its predecessor, a novel in which Italy provides a setting for a social world that is cosmopolitan and that ranges over a large part of the scale of human iniquity, from adultery to terrorism and from blackmail to murder. Like some of the earlier novels it shares some of the preoccupations of the thriller, carrying them to such lengths that the thriller genre is parodied but at the same time insisting that in the world of the 1970s this is what 'real life' is like: it is only in such fiction as that represented by Anthea Leaver's library book that the pretence can be kept up that 'personal relationships' are all-important.

Ultimately, however, Muriel Spark is less interested in crime than in evil, and the point is made in *Territorial Rights* that a certain kind of human being delights in doing evil: Coleridge spoke of Iago's 'motiveless malignity', and Muriel Spark's Venice has something in common with Shakespeare's in *Othello*, though its comedy and satire, as well as its fascination with wealth and the power of money and greed, make it closer to Ben Jonson's *Volpone*, another classic drama set in Venice. Near the end of the novel the naive Anthea Leaver, whose placid Birmingham existence has kept her from the knowledge of what people can be capable of, expresses her relief, saying of her husband that she ' "was always afraid he was unhappy and involved in some wrong-doing" '. Anthea's assumption that vice leads to misery is corrected by Grace, an ex-school matron: ' "You're mistaken if you think wrong-doers are always unhappy," Grace said. "The really professional evil-doers love it. They're as happy as larks in the sky. I wasn't a Matron all those years without finding out a thing or two about human nature" ' (p. 235 in the 1979 edition). As such figures as Georgina Hogg and Patrick Seton attest, Muriel Spark had always had an interest in 'professional evil-doers', but by this stage in her career their doings loom much larger and colour the tone of the whole novel.

Territorial Rights follows *Not to Disturb*, *The Takeover*, and other novels of this period, however, in declining to take an explicit stand on the moral issues it raises. A world of vice, crime and sin is depicted, as in the sensational press, without moral comment. As Ruth Whittaker puts it, there is 'an exuberant air of deliberate superficiality, a refusal, almost, to engage profoundly in moral issues. . . . Like Evelyn Waugh, [Muriel Spark] has withdrawn to a high and distant viewing platform from which she chronicles the activities of the world as she sees them'.[72]

A Muriel Spark novel contrives to be simultaneously unmistakable and unpredictable: each bears the imprint of her idiosyncratic manner and resembles nothing but the other novels of the same author, and yet one can never be quite sure what she will do next. Her art is *sui generis*, defining its own terms, and one often feels not only that she is discarding much of what has been achieved by earlier novelists but that many of her own novels represent, as T. S. Eliot said of poetry, a wholly new beginning. And yet she is an inveterate self-imitator, taking up again in later novels characters, situations, ideas, and motifs that have appeared earlier. The easy-going and self-delighting mood of *Loitering with Intent* does not make it an obvious successor to the severe works that immediately preceded it, but it initiates a process (to be continued in the later *A Far Cry from Kensington*) of revisiting: theme, setting, period and narrative technique all hark back to novels written near the beginning of her career. It is perhaps going too far, or not far enough, to describe it (as Alan Bold does) as an 'autobiographical novel',[73] but one has a sense of the writer, after a quarter of a century dedicated to the art of fiction, looking back on her own life and career.

Many writers (and not a few who are not writers) do this in the later stages of a long career, and the impulse commonly manifests itself in the composition of an autobiography. Muriel Spark was 63 in the year in which *Loitering with Intent* appeared: that is the age that astrologers called the Grand Climacteric (the multiple of the magic numbers of seven and three threes); it was traditionally associated with the natural end of existence; and Muriel Spark's interest in numerology suggests that she can hardly have been unaware of the significance of this phase of her own life. What she gives us is a novel that opens in a graveyard and ends with the protagonist reflecting that, 'having entered the fullness of my years, from there by the grace of God I go on my way rejoicing'. The last phrase occurs several times in the novel, but before she can go on her way she must, as the title hints, loiter or linger, not idly but purposefully or 'with intent'.

Like *Robinson*, her second novel, it is a first-person narrative – not a form that the less personal novels of the intervening years could have tolerated (*The Driver's Seat*, for instance, would be unthinkable in this narrative mode). Like *The Comforters*, her first, it concerns a heroine who is writing a novel. And like several of the early books it returns, now over a longer space, to mid-century London: the time and place of the author's own youth and literary beginnings. The opening pages show the narrator-protagonist 'in the Kensington area of London' 'One day in the middle of the twentieth century', and at the beginning of the final chapter she returns to this point, now specifying the date as Friday, 30 June 1950.[74] The main action occupies the ten months preceding this date: it begins in September 1949, in Chapter 2 it is October, by Chapter 5 (when Fleur finishes her novel) it is January 1950, and so on. We have had other occasions to note Muriel Spark's fondness for a precise time scheme even when it accommodates mystery or fantasy.

When the book opens, Fleur Talbot, a young woman, is sitting in the graveyard writing a poem. She is also, it turns out, writing an autobiographical novel, *Warrender Chase*, 'without any great hope of ever getting it published, but with only the excited compulsion to write it' (Bodley Head edition, 1981, p. 25). But the first-person account of the young Fleur is written at a much later stage of her life, when she has become an established novelist; and the account itself is described as an 'autobiography' (p. 25). Already, then, a number of complex relationships have been set up: of the young Fleur to the older Fleur, of both to the author (or perhaps to the author at different stages of *her* life), and of autobiography to fiction.

This last relationship is crucial and, again, looks back to *The Comforters*: the nature of fictional 'truth', the relationship of 'reality' to fiction, the connection between fictional characters and the real-life persons on whom they may be based, or who, alternatively, may be found to, or may come to, resemble them – these problems are again explored, though with an assurance and sophistication not to be found (and hardly to be expected) in the earlier work.

Needing employment while she finishes her first novel, Fleur is hired by Sir Quentin Oliver, who runs an organisation called the Autobiographical Association. (Muriel Spark's work with the Poetry Society is an obvious though far from precise parallel.) Sir Quentin encourages members to submit their memoirs to him, for publication long after their death; this provides him with opportunities for blackmail. Fleur's task is to type them, and she enlivens this routine by polishing up, or fictionalising, the material. (The idea is an extended version of the liberties taken by Dougal in *The Ballad of Peckham Rye*.) She has found a way, in a word, of turning autobiographers into novelists; we may reflect at this point that Fleur herself is both a novelist and a character in an autobiographical fiction. Put slightly differently, the 'real' authors of the memoirs are turned into characters in fictions – which in any case they are already, of course. Fleur's work on the memoirs also, as she says, 'feeds my imagination for my novel *Warrender Chase*', another kind of connection between fact and fiction. The recurrent interest in plotting is once again evident: Sir Quentin's sinister plots have a relationship to the plot-making of Fleur the novelist ('So that his purposes were quite different from mine, yet at the same time they coincided . . .': p. 37).

As this crude outline may serve to suggest, Muriel Spark has created a simple yet subtle and highly suggestive situation that will enable her to investigate problems of art and reality. Matters become more complex when Fleur first begins to regard the 'real-life' subjects of the memoirs as 'characters of my own', like the characters in the novel she is writing – she has, after all, largely 'created' them as literary entities – and then finds that life imitates her fictions. The reader has been prepared for this from an early stage:

The process by which I created my characters was instinctive,
the sum of my whole experience of others and of my own
potential self; and so it always has been. Sometimes I don't
actually meet a character I have created in a novel until some
time after the novel has been written and published. (pp. 24–
5)

More than one critic has pointed out that the second of these
sentences is almost a self-quotation, for Muriel Spark had told
Malcolm Muggeridge in a television interview in 1961 that
'sometimes I invent a character that I meet later on after the
book is written'. A more generalised way of putting this would
be to say that fiction can tell truths that we recognise *as* truths
only later on in our experience of actuality. In the action of the
novel Fleur first kills off the hero of her novel in a car crash and
then finds that the 'real' Sir Quentin, who has come more and
more to resemble the fictional (doubly fictional) Warrender
Chase, suffers a similar fate. The traditional assumptions of
realist fiction, that the novel is a mirror or working model of life
copied more or less faithfully from an original, is neatly reversed.
Fleur's novel is not a copy of life as she has observed it but a
part of God's master-plan for human destinies.

It is fair to assume that this view of the autonomy and self-
sufficiency of art represents Muriel Spark's own conception of
the nature of fiction, and her own assessment of its importance.
The novel contains many passages that declare her own stance
on questions of literary aesthetics. For instance, when a friend
suggests that one of the characters in her book is 'evil', Fleur
objects:

'How can you say that? Marjorie is fiction, she doesn't exist.'
'Marjorie is a personification of evil.'
'What is a personification?' I said. 'Marjorie is only words.'
(pp. 73–4)

And on the impersonality of art:

I wasn't writing poetry and prose so that the reader would
think me a nice person, but in order that my sets of words
should convey ideas of truth and wonder, as indeed they did
to myself as I was composing them. (p. 82)

Some of these statements are uttered in what seems very close to an authorial voice:

> Since the story of my own life is just as much constituted of the secrets of my craft as it is of other events, I might as well remark here that to make a character ring true it needs must be in some way contradictory, somewhere a paradox. (p. 41)

Ruth Whittaker has commented that the protagonist 'seems closely to resemble Mrs Spark herself, and many of her pronouncements on writing are echoes, almost word for word, of statements made by Mrs Spark in interviews'.[75]

Not for the first time, Muriel Spark has written in *Loitering with Intent* a novel about the novel, a fiction that not merely draws attention to its own fictiveness but explores different layers or levels of fictiveness and questions customary assumptions about the relationships between them. Just as Fleur, touching up the memoirs written by the 'real' members of the Autobiographical Association, comes to think of them as 'inventions of my own', she expresses the artist's solipsistic or God-like sense of being responsible for the universe:

> It then came to me again, there in the taxi, what a wonderful thing it was to be a woman and an artist in the twentieth century. It was almost as if Sir Quentin was unreal and I had merely invented him, Warrender Chase being a man, a real man on whom I had partly based Sir Quentin. (p. 183)

The joke here, a serious joke, depends upon the pronoun 'I' as well as on words like 'unreal' and 'invented': the unreal, invented Fleur is worrying about the unreality of the invented Sir Quentin. But if Sir Quentin is unreal, what is Warrender Chase? Paradoxically, less unreal, since 'real' characters, it is demonstrated, can come to resemble fictions.

The paragraph from which the last quotation was taken concludes with the following sentence: 'It is true that I felt tight-strung, but I remember those sensations very clearly', and Fleur's 'tight-strung' quality is several times referred to. Sometimes it is explained as a light-headedness that is one of the after-effects of influenza, but sometimes it sounds more like anxiety, neurosis

or mental instability. There is a striking passage in which Fleur
tells her friend Dottie that

> Sir Quentin was conforming more and more to the character
> of my Warrender Chase; it was amazing, I could have invented
> him, I could have invented all of them – the lot. (p. 106)

Dottie expresses the opinion, understandable enough, that she
is 'unhinged' and 'suffering from delusions', and before dismissing
this quickly as a failure to comprehend the nature of the artist
it is possible to speculate on what might follow if Dottie's
diagnosis were accurate. If the unstable Fleur *had* invented
the implausible-sounding Autobiographical Association and its
members, that would be no more than an extension of her role
as a maker of fictions. And, extending speculation even further,
since we in any case have (as usual in autobiographical fiction)
only Fleur's word for anything, suppose everything in her story
were an invention – as of course on another level it is. (The
unreliable autobiographer, in such works as Nabokov's *Pale Fire*
(1962), is a familiar figure in modern fiction.) Further yet, taking
up the hint at the outset with its graveyard setting, is it
conceivable that Fleur speaks from beyond the grave and hence
has access to God's plots to an extent not enjoyed by living
women, even novelists? This can be no more than speculation,
though we shall want to return to it in discussing *A Far Cry from
Kensington*. 'Loitering with intent', though, is not a bad description
of ghostly habits, and without quite reaching this point Alan
Bold seems to move in the same direction when he speaks of
Fleur 'purposively haunting the earth while possessed by creative
vitality'.[76]

Of the creative vitality there can be no doubt. Fleur's name
suggests freshness, with perhaps a side-glance at Muriel Spark's
favourite Proust[77](and her own novel may fairly be labelled a
remembrance of and quest for things past). She has a relaxed
narrative style that is often colloquial, almost gossipy, but
sometimes touches lyricism, as when she says 'I was aware of a
daemon inside me that rejoiced in seeing people as they were, and
not only that, but more than ever as they were, and more, and
more' (p. 9). Her conversational style occasionally admits an
unexpected exotic such as *orgulous* or introduces a variation on a
trite phrase, as when she says 'I have always been on the listen-

in for those sort of phrases' (p. 13), the freshly minted 'listen-in' ousting the expected 'look-out'. These are, of course, stylistic mannerisms of Muriel Spark herself, as is the trick of ending a sentence with a sudden shift in tone or register: 'At that time I had a number of marvellous friends, full of good and evil' (p. 9), the banality of 'marvellous friends' leaving the reader quite unprepared for the seriousness of the final phrase. Compare, from *Memento Mori*: 'three other grannies . . . who had been attached to Granny Barnacle in various ways, including those of love, hate, scorn, resentment, and pity', and the concluding sentence of *The Driver's Seat*. What this adds up to is that Muriel Spark has taken no ventriloquial pains to endow her heroine-narrator with an idiosyncratic 'voice'; nor is this to be expected in a novel which is so largely autobiographical.

The autobiographical note, however, is hardly the right one on which to conclude this discussion, for *Loitering with Intent* is a remarkable and exhilarating examination of the nature of the novelist's art and a spirited urging of the high seriousness of fiction. It is characteristic that this enterprise should be conducted not through works of conventional autobiography or criticism but through fiction itself – fiction that examines, entirely without pretensions or portentousness, but with deep seriousness, its own nature and purpose.

There are at least two kinds of literariness in Muriel Spark's fiction: a relationship, often parodic, to an established genre, often of a popular kind, such as the detective story (*The Driver's Seat*) or the school story (*The Prime of Miss Jean Brodie*), and a relationship to a specific and familiar text (*Robinson*). Her seventeenth novel, *The Only Problem*, belongs to the second category: like her first novel, *The Comforters*, it makes use of her long-standing interest in the Book of Job,[78] and the 'only problem' is the problem of suffering in a world created by God. This time, however, the relationship between the novel and the Old Testament text is more intimate and more problematic; it is also complicated by the use made of another work of art, the painting 'Job visited by his wife' by the seventeenth-century French artist Georges de la Tour, reproduced on the jacket of the original edition. This painting is to be found at Epinal in the Vosges, and it is in that part of France that much of the action takes place.

The Only Problem is not the first modern novel to make use of
the Book of Job. Joseph Roth's starkly powerful *Job: The Story of
a Simple Man* (originally published in 1930 in German as *Hiob,
Roman eines einfachen Mannes*; translated into English, 1933)
narrates the fortunes and misfortunes of a Russian Jew who
struggles to bring up his family, leaves his homeland to emigrate
to New York, suffers much sorrow, but at last is made happy by
a seeming miracle. Roth's Mendel Singer resembles the biblical
Job in being visited by severe trials of his faith and at last
achieving peace and prosperity; he differs from him in being
miserably poor, for Job was a rich man at both the beginning
and the end of the story.

Muriel Spark's Harvey Gotham is a Canadian millionaire who
is preoccupied, even obsessed, with the story of Job and is writing
a book on the subject (as Muriel Spark herself seems at one time
to have intended to do). At many points in the novel the reader
seems to be invited to make a connection between Harvey and
Job: the former is rich, in Part II he is afflicted with troubles
(though not with boils) and is visited by various comforters, and
in the closing words of the book he answers an enquiry as to
what he will do now by saying, ' "Live another hundred and
forty years. I'll have three daughters, Clara, Jemima and Eye-
Paint" ' – a reference to the ending of the Book of Job (we have
earlier been told that the name of one of Job's daughters, Keren-
happuch, means Box of Eye-Paint). Like Caroline Rose in *The
Comforters*, Harvey is writing a book as well as taking part in
one, and the novel ends when, or at the same time as, he finishes
his monograph.

There are other passages in which our attention is explicitly
directed towards the biblical Job. At the end of Chapter 7, for
instance, Harvey asks a visitor ' ". . . what are you doing here?" '
and receives the reply: ' "I suppose I'm just a comforter" ' (1984
edition, p. 121). Later, when Harvey is told of the murder of a
policeman in Paris and asked whether the victim's wife 'deserved'
to have this tragedy inflicted upon her, he replies:

'No. . . . Neither did the policeman. We do not get what
we merit. The one thing has nothing to do with the other. . . .
(p. 144)

– a reference to the main theme of the Job story, unmerited

suffering. And, as he contemplates the de la Tour painting on one of his many visits to the museum, Harvey recalls 'the verses that followed the account of Job's afflictions with boils' (p. 77). The painting itself is the subject of a long set-piece description (pp. 75–8) that is also a meditation upon its meaning.

There are, however, difficulties in the way of seeing Harvey as a modern Job. There is a good supply of appalling happenings in the novel, including murder, robbery, and terrorist activity, but these events, though they concern people closely connected to Harvey, do not seem to touch him very deeply. Events like the placing of a bomb in a supermarket and the shooting of a policeman have a contemporary flavour, and Muriel Spark may be saying that these are the forms that tribulations are liable to take in the modern world: the nature of the troubles is as different from those of Job as Harvey's wealth is, in modern capitalist society, from the patriarch's flocks and herds. Even so, a case can be made out for seeing Harvey as a cold and self-centred intellectual, incapable of suffering or of feeling for the sufferings of others. This is certainly the view of Alan Bold, who believes that 'His insight into Job's predicament is an intellectual affectation', that he 'eschews evil only because it has never visited him', and that he has 'rejected reality in the interests of his academic isolationism'.[79]

There is certainly a marked contrast between the two worlds depicted in the novel. Harvey is cocooned by wealth (a now familiar interest of Muriel Spark's) and lives, physically isolated, in retreat from the world of action, immersed in his scholarly researches and in the brooding contemplation of two works of art, a poem and a picture. Outside is a world of ideologies, fanaticisms, violence and death. The chief representative of the latter is Harvey's wife Effie, whose political passions lead her to join a gang of terrorists. Harvey's decision to leave her is abrupt and is precipitated by an apparently trivial prank: when they stop at a motorway shop she steals two bars of chocolate, justifying her action with the remark that it is proper to seize the property of capitalists who are themselves responsible for a world in which huge numbers of people are starving. For Harvey this moment seems to constitute a vision of evil comparable to that seen by Nicholas in *The Girls of Slender Means*, and Effie's conduct proves him right, for she joins a terrorist group called the Front for the Liberation of Europe and is eventually killed.

All this is, of course, a long way from the Book of Job, where, as Frank Kermode points out, a mere two verses out of 42 chapters are devoted to Job's wife. In the painting, however, which is clearly of great importance in Muriel Spark's novel, Job's wife not only appears, but dominates the group. Harvey is aware that this constitutes a problem of interpretation, since there seems to be no biblical authority for the scene depicted. At the same time he instinctively feels that the painting may provide a clue to the understanding of the literary work:

> To Harvey's mind there was much more in the painting to illuminate the subject of Job than in many of the lengthy commentaries that he knew so well. It was eloquent of a new idea, and yet where had the painter found justification for his treatment of the subject? . . .
>
> The scene here seemed to Harvey so altogether different from that suggested by the text of *Job*, and yet so deliberately and intelligently contemplated that it was impossible not to wonder what the artist actually meant. . . . (pp. 76–7)

Harvey's response to the painting may furnish a clue to solving another problem of interpretation, the meaning of Muriel Spark's novel. For here too we seem to have a 'version' of the Job story that does not (as Joseph Roth's novel does) follow it fairly closely but departs from it substantially and in puzzling ways. If the significance of the painting depends on Job's wife, then the significance of the novel may depend upon Harvey's wife; and Effie's conduct may be intended to illustrate a peculiarly modern form of evil, a shallow and modish fanaticism that is the reverse of true faith.

Frank Kermode's long and interesting review of *The Only Problem* (*London Review of Books*, 20 September–3 October 1984) draws attention to an ambiguity or problem of interpretation in the ancient poem that we call the Book of Job. The advice given by Job's wife to her husband means literally, in the Hebrew version, 'Bless God and die', and this is literally translated in the Vulgate (Latin) version ('benedic Deo'). It is often held, however, that what she *means* is 'Curse God and die', and such a meaning fits better with Job's reply to her: 'Thou speakest as one of the foolish women speaketh. What? Shall we receive good

at the hand of God, and shall we not receive evil?' If we apply
this to Harvey's wife, there is a sense in which the 'message' of
Effie's actions is that life is too terrible for belief in a loving
Creator to be possible – but to the believer, and especially to
the student of the Book of Job, this is a 'foolish' doctrine, since
human life without evil as well as good would be morally insipid.

The Only Problem is a recent novel and we ought not to be
surprised if its interpretation is not a simple and effortless
matter. It represents the fruits of many years' interest in the
Book of Job, allied to many years spent in the making of fictions,
and the relationship of novel to source could hardly be other
than a subtle one. Yet Muriel Spark must also have been
conscious of engaging in a familiar and time-honoured activity,
for as Frank Kermode reminds us, 'Making up stories in order
to update or explain older stories, to make sense of them under
altered conditions, is a highly traditional activity, and treating
Old Testament stories thus is a practice going back at least to
the New Testament'. Kermode also speculates on what might
have been the origins of the book:

> If there were a Spark Notebook, like Henry James's, an
> imaginable entry might run: 'Suppose that in our time some
> rich man were not only deep in the study of Job but himself
> in a situation of – well, shall I say discomfort, interested in
> the vague analogy between himself and his subject? Something
> might be made of it. Remember Georges de la Tour's *Job
> Visited by his Wife*.' Between the large general idea and the
> beautiful and blest nouvelle (which is what this writer does
> best) lie many questions as to how the thing is to be done,
> many scenarios perhaps. And in the development of these
> notions it would seem that the painting played a large part.

The Only Problem harshly evokes the 'altered conditions' of the
contemporary world – as in *Territorial Rights* and elsewhere, it is
Europe, and specifically Italy, that is the scene of acts of
ruthless crime – and summons the ancient text in an attempt to
make sense of a world in which such things are possible. In the
event the relationship between the ancient and modern texts is
not vague but oblique, complex and teasing, and mediated
through a third work of art, the de la Tour painting.

The finality of the ending perhaps marks not merely the

conclusion of this book but the end of a major phase of Muriel
Spark's fiction, though it would obviously be rash to be dogmatic
on this point. If this is the case, it is a phase that comprises nine
novels that occupied her over a period of twenty years. A note
of summing up was undeniably discernible in some of the reviews,
and at least two distinguished critics took the opportunity to try
to 'place' her, and were prepared to make large claims for her
achievement. Kermode wrote, 'I do indeed think of her as our
best novelist', observing at the same time that some obvious
features of her work lead to her being 'not classed with the
heavies' and hence to her being frequently undervalued or even
disparaged. Gabriel Josipovici opened his review (*Times Literary
Supplement*, 7 September 1984) by saying that her novels are 'a
joy to read and a nightmare to talk about', but was willing to
conclude three long columns later with the declaration that 'she
is the best English novelist writing today'.

5

Back to the Fifties

A Far Cry from Kensington (1988) is Muriel Spark's eighteenth novel and, at the time of writing, her most recent. It appeared in the year in which its author was seventy: the biblical three score years and ten, and a time of life at which many people, if they have survived so far, may want to take stock of the past. Many writers in their old age show an anxiety to put their literary affairs in order as well as coming to terms with their personal lives: they write autobiographies, produce collected editions of their works, sort (and perhaps burn) papers. A few extend this process into works of art: Hardy in *The Well-Beloved* constructs an allegory of the artist's life, Graham Greene in *Travels with my Aunt* writes a picaresque comedy filled with motifs from his own earlier books, William Golding in *The Paper Men* shows an elderly writer grappling with the intrusions of a would-be biographer.

It is too early to be dogmatic about the meaning of *A Far Cry from Kensington*, on which light may be shed by other books its author will publish (and one hopes they will be numerous) in the years ahead. But it seems possible that this is a novel which draws upon the author's own earlier books, borrowing a theme, a character or a situation from here and there[80] and devising from them a story that is to some extent nostalgic, even self-indulgent, but that also, as the title insists, squarely faces the distance that lies, in personal and social terms, between the recreated world and the world in which it is recreated. It is not the successor to *The Only Problem* that one might have expected (and it may be significant that the interval between the two books is longer than at any other point in Muriel Spark's career), but it is not as different from her earlier work as some accounts of it suggest. Probably one ought not to expect criticism, or even accuracy, from a publisher's blurb, but the dust jacket's claim

111

that it is 'delectable, funny and stylish' and 'perfectly evokes London in the '50s, and in particular the world of the vanished Kensington bedsitters' seems rather determinedly to miss the point. Not much closer to the mark are the comments of one distinguished reviewer, Anita Brookner, who commends its 'lightheartedness, even its banality', the 'charm' of the central character, and the 'happy ending' (*Spectator*, 26 March 1988). If this were all there is, there would be grounds for fearing that Muriel Spark had gone soft.

In fact the novel has a substantial moral, even a theological, dimension, and those who know her earlier work will be aware that this can coexist with, and not be undermined by, the wit and humour, the sharp social observation and sense of place and period. Anita Brookner's perhaps unintentionally disparaging conclusion that the novel provides 'an incidental pleasure, one that will keep us going contentedly until the next instalment of Muriel Spark's true genius is vouchsafed to us' leaves out of account the fact that, like *The Only Problem* and many earlier works, it is concerned with evil as manifested in everyday life. If there are angels dining at the Ritz, there can be also devils going about their business in offices and pubs.

The period of the action is 1954–5. That is, of course, the period in which some of Muriel Spark's earliest novels were set, and it was clearly a crucial period in her own life. By 1988, however, it was a long way off, just as the author, long resident in Italy, is a 'far cry' from the London in which she spent her youth. The period now has to be recreated, as if in a historical novel: coffee bars are opening up, Roger Bannister runs the first four-minute mile, the A-line dress is fashionable, the 'Red Dean' (a churchman with Communist sympathies, once a favourite of journalists and now almost forgotten) is in the news. It is in short the world of *The Comforters* and *The Bachelors*, now no longer a contemporary world but thirty years on.

The novel opens in 1954 (p. 6: all page references to the 1988 edition); an epilogue, set 'more than thirty years later' (p. 188), brings the time of narration very close to, if not coincident with, the date of composition. The first-person narrative is in the hands of Mrs Hawkins, who is at its outset a young war widow living in a rooming-house in South Kensington, presided over by its owner, Milly, another widow and an Irish Catholic. Among the other occupants are Wanda, a Polish refugee who is also a widow and a Catholic and carries on the profession of dressmaker in her room; an attractive young secretary, Isobel, who leads a busy social life; Kate Parker, a district nurse obsessed with hygiene; and the Carlins, a married couple. There is also William Todd, a medical student, whom Mrs Hawkins marries at the end of the book. It is very much a house of women (and of widows, especially Catholic widows), and the atmosphere of camaraderie and neighbourliness recalls *The Girls of Slender Means*. Mrs Hawkins, however, is far from being slender: enormously fat, she follows a successful diet in the course of the story that reduces her to normal proportions – as the book grows, she gets smaller.

Into this society of individuals bound together by proximity and friendliness, a kind of lay community, comes evil that shatters the idyll, for Wanda receives first an anonymous letter and then menacing phone calls (the anonymous and disembodied voice recalling such early novels as *The Comforters* and *Memento Mori*). The effect upon her is profound, and at last she commits suicide. In order to understand this tragic development we need to bear in mind the narrator's professional life. She works for a series of small publishing firms and in the course of her work encounters a writer, Hector Bartlett, to whom she takes an intense and apparently irrational dislike. The fact that he is a bad writer and an unpleasant man hardly seems to justify the one-woman campaign she directs against him. Recalling the phrase 'pisseur de copie' (almost untranslatable, but meaning roughly 'one who pisses manuscripts', i.e. produces inferior work in an effortless stream), which she has encountered in connection with a French author, she hisses it at him whenever she meets him, and uses it of him to others.[81] Like her dislike, his reaction seems excessive: he plans an elaborate revenge, involving Wanda, and Wanda's deep anxiety and eventual suicide stem at least partly from her conviction that, by practising a kind of black magic, she is causing Mrs Hawkins to pine away. (Actually, as the reader is well aware, she is losing weight by scrupulously observing her diet.)

How can we account for Mrs Hawkins's antipathy to Hector Bartlett? When a friend expresses regret that she has to refer to him as 'the *Pisseur*', she replies: ' "I can't help it. Sometimes the words just come out and I can't stop them. It feels like preaching the gospel" ' (p. 110). This seems to suggest that Mrs Hawkins recognises Bartlett as evil and is impelled by some non-rational power from within herself to denounce him. It is, however, apparently contradicted by her later statement that '"here in England love and hate are two entirely different things. They are not even opposites. According to my outlook, love comes in the first place from the heart and hate arises basically from principle"' (pp. 136–7). Whether from instinct or principle, though, she perceives Bartlett as evil. Like other devil-figures from Dickens's Fagin to Muriel Spark's own Dougal Douglas, he has red hair. But his actual deeds seem to represent diabolism in a very mild form: in a pub, for instance, he puts mustard on a sausage and offers it to a dog – hardly the action of an animal lover, but surely falling short of pure evil. As in *The Girls of Slender Means*, however, Muriel Spark may be making the point that evil, like goodness, can be manifested in the banalities of everyday life. For Nicholas in the earlier novel, the rescue of the Schiaparelli dress was a diabolical act; for Mrs Hawkins too the devil can pursue his business in South Kensington, and she needs must denounce him when she meets him. As another reviewer, Nigel Andrew, has said, '[Bartlett's] evil presence is in fact the key to the whole narrative' (*The Listener*, 24 March 1988).

This kind of situation is not, however, precisely new in Muriel Spark's fiction, and the question arises whether *A Far Cry from Kensington* is breaking new ground or may simply be regarded as a late, nostalgic and affectionate reworking of material from her earlier work, a kind of revisiting of the author's own creative past. Certainly it seems to break the series of detached accounts of the hollowness of the contemporary world that extends, with only a couple of interruptions, from *The Public Image* to *The Only Problem*, and to forsake the international scene for a familiar and beloved place. It also seems to return to the autobiographical mode of some of the early books, with a sprightly and engaging heroine whose personal and professional situation bears some obvious resemblances to those of the author herself in the Fifties.

At this point we should recall that Muriel Spark's long career has shown her to have a considerable capacity for surprising her readers and critics, and it would be unwise to jump to conclusions about a novel that may only yield its full meaning on repeated rereadings and perhaps in the light of other novels that may follow it. When William Golding's *The Paper Men* appeared in 1984, some reviewers found it trivial and banal, and disappointment was widespread. One reviewer, however, more cautious and possibly wiser than the rest, issued a warning, and since he himself is a distinguished novelist with a long career behind him it ought not to be ignored. Anthony Burgess wrote of *The Paper Men*:

> When a piece of fiction seems banal but its author is distinguished and universally honoured, we are compelled to take second and third looks at it, prepared to be convinced that the banality is a kind of code or a new mode of profundity or elegance we are too stupid to perceive. (*The Observer*, 5 February 1984)

These words can be, and perhaps should be, applied, without changing a syllable, to Muriel Spark's latest novel. The fact that it is an easy read – 'After the rigours of *The Only Problem*', said Nigel Andrew, 'Muriel Spark has this time slipped into something more comfortable' – may be deceptive. So may be the fact that the heroine-narrator is such an agreeable and companionable lady. The trouble with a first-person narrative is that the reader is furnished with no check upon the narrator's veracity, and that includes her self-portrait: the unreliable narrator is a familiar phenomenon in modern fiction, and Mrs Hawkins's easygoing, unpretentious charm may be a trap set for the reader by the novelist.

Such a possibility could even accommodate a situation that may sound far-fetched. The narrator does a lot of her remembering of the past as she lies awake in bed, in the dark, in the silence. To use the words of a poem that Muriel Spark herself quotes from, the grave's a fine and private place: suppose that the mind that evokes the past belongs to one who is dead? It is true that some elements in the novel, including the epilogue, seem to make this a difficult reading to accept. But it would give an even sharper and more wistful point to the title, as well as to the fact that the heroine married a man called Todd – a name that has exactly the same sound as the German for death. The essential point, though, is that Muriel Spark's eighteenth novel may eventually be seen very differently from the way in which it has struck its earliest readers, and all we know of this writer should make such an outcome no matter for surprise.

6

Postscript

I have called the final section of this book a postscript and not
a conclusion because claims of conclusiveness where the work of
a living writer is concerned seem impertinent, if not fraudulent.
There may be more novels to come, and they may not only pose
fresh problems but suggest new ways of looking at the novels we
already have. In any case there is as yet no consensus on Muriel
Spark's standing as a novelist: while there are those who regard
her as the best living British writer of fiction, there are also those
who prefer to stress her limitations. So that critical judgements,
always provisional and for the time being, must be even more
so than usual.

Nevertheless (to use the word that, recalling her Edinburgh
childhood, she has identified as embodying a principle on which
'much of my literary composition is based'),[82] the shape of her
career so far seems reasonably clear. One view of it, at least, is
reflected in the structure of the present book. After a relatively
late start as a novelist she wrote and published seven novels
very rapidly, as if drawing on a large accumulated store of
experience, including mental experience. We have her own word
for it that they were written rapidly; also that, having once
begun, she enjoyed the security and confidence that came of
having made up her mind on all the issues that really matter.
These are for the most part novels of a particular time and place
(the exceptions are *Robinson*, an island story, and *The Prime of
Miss Jean Brodie*, which moves north from London to Edinburgh
and back from the postwar period to the thirties); they are all
short, self-denying in the succinctness of their descriptive and
dialogue elements, somewhat limited in their characterisation,
but generous in their complexities of plot. Many of them show
an interest in the processes and problems of fiction making, both
the formal fictions of the novelist and the often unacknowledged

fictions that we all encounter and generate in our daily lives. And some of them combine a familiar and even banal surface realism with intrusions of fantasy or the supernatural: a character has vestigial horns on his head; Death makes anonymous telephone calls.

The Mandelbaum Gate, however, seems to represent a disinclination to continue in the vein so successfully established, or perhaps a response to doubts whether novels so slight, bright and light deserved to be taken seriously. She told Frank Kermode, in an interview cited earlier, that she had no ambitions to be considered 'Mrs. Tolstoy', but she is unlikely to have been gratified by the reputation for being a purveyor of sophisticated entertainment that was earned in some quarters by the success of her books in the early sixties. *The Mandelbaum Gate* is her attempt at writing a substantial, rather traditional novel, and she does not seem to have been particularly pleased by the result. Certainly she did not repeat the experiment; instead her work takes an entirely different direction with *The Public Image* and its successors, which return to the novella form favoured earlier (Muriel Spark shares Henry James's partiality for what he called 'the beautiful and blessed nouvelle'). Now, however, the settings are not London or Edinburgh but Italy, Switzerland and New York. (Again there are exceptions: *The Abbess of Crewe* is a topical and not very successful satire, *Loitering with Intent* an autobiographical narrative that returns to the place and time of the early books.)

This second group of novels contrasts with the first in another way: instead of depicting a middle-class Britain in which, despite the presence of eccentrics, frauds, the criminal and the ungodly, the circumstances of life are reasonably secure, she now turns to a larger world in which violence is liable to erupt in the form of murder, suicide, terrorism, or large-scale financial chicanery. Instead of the impoverished or mildly affluent Londoners of the early novels, the characters are now drawn from a rich and rootless international set. The earlier interest in fiction making in daily life now manifests itself specifically in a preoccupation with the power of the mass media and the distasteful fictions of journalists and film-makers. Only in *A Far Cry from Kensington* does this world seem to be left behind.

Muriel Spark's novels are often spoken of as if they were modern morality plays and as if their theological aspects were paramount, but it is as well to remember that her novels of the

seventies can also be viewed as reflecting the changing political
and economic climate of the period. A passage in *The Takeover* is
relevant:

> At dinner they spoke of Hubert, and of Nemi to where they
> were all planning shortly to return. It was not in their minds
> at the time that this last quarter of the year they had entered,
> that of 1973, was in fact the beginning of something new in their
> world; a change in the meaning of property and money. . . . it
> did not occur to one of those spirited and in various ways
> intelligent people round Berto's table that a complete mutation
> of our means of nourishment had already come into being
> where the concept of money and property were concerned, a
> complete mutation not merely to be defined as a collapse of
> the capitalist system, or a global recession, but such a sea-
> change in the nature of reality as could not have been envisaged
> by Karl Marx or Sigmund Freud. Such a mutation that what
> were assets were to be liabilities and no armed guards could
> be found and fed sufficient to guard those armed guards who
> failed to protect the properties they guarded, whether hoarded
> in banks or built on confined territories, whether they were
> priceless works of art, or merely hieroglyphics registered in
> the computers. (pp. 126–7)

The hard contemporary world of these novels finds a fitting
emblem in the geometrical rigidities and cold impersonality of
the furniture in Lise's Copenhagen apartment in *The Driver's
Seat*; the brief lyrical allusions to the swaying forests from which
the wood has come remind us of what such a world has lost or
renounced. Narrative method and narrative tone also suffer a
sea-change in these later books: the serene and jaunty, often
witty or nostalgic, manner of the London novels is exchanged
for the impersonal, rather severe style of a recording instrument
(and, in some instances, for a use of the present tense that largely
precludes perspective or explicit judgement).

Considering her work as a whole, or as much of a whole as
has so far been vouchsafed to us, some have found her claims to
be taken seriously only too easy to resist, and it is worth enquiring
why this should be so. She is, to our gain but her own possible
disadvantage, a very entertaining writer, consistently 'readable'
(to use that last refuge of fainthearted praise), and this very

accessibility may raise suspicions if not hackles. In the strange dichotomy of much academic discussion 'popular' is opposed to 'serious', and Muriel Spark's accessibility has been taken as signalling a want of body and depth. Her most distinguished critic answered this point ten years ago. Reviewing *Territorial Rights*, Frank Kermode wrote that

> we should by now have learned how to read her. But although we may know the kind of response required of us, we shall always, with each new book, have to deal with a very specific problem, not always easy to identify. . . . If the story seems to be superficial or to be lacking in point, we can be fairly sure that we are reading it lazily or naively. The great pleasures offered by this writer are contingent upon our being willing to work harder than usual. (*Listener*, 26 April 1979)

Kermode also reminds us that the sense of sameness, of her having written the same book over and over again, is illusory: a casual reading may suggest as much, but a closer scrutiny shows new problems, aesthetic and moral, at work in the familiar settings, character types or plot devices.

The fact remains, however, that Muriel Spark disappoints, and in all likelihood deliberately disappoints, many readers' expectations of what a 'serious' or 'important' novel should offer. The brevity, almost amounting to perfunctoriness; the emphasis on comedy, even farce, and the fondness for parody; the lack of interest in psychological complexity, in motivation, in character development, these traditional responsibilities incurred by the novelist's vocation – all of these may be regarded as weighty objections. Added to this is the problem that even her warmest admirers might find it difficult to nominate any one of her novels for the accolade of 'major novel'.

One response might be that it is irrelevant to judge by criteria derived from the traditional novel a writer who has from the start made clear her own tough-minded independence of, even indifference to, most of what constitutes the English tradition of fiction. It is relevant that, while widely and deeply read in the poets, she is not much interested in other people's novels and shows no sign of having read many of them. The few influences on her work among writers of prose fiction are the dandies and fantasists Beerbohm and Firbank and the poets James Hogg and

Emily Brontë. She has written no *Middlemarch* because she does
not conceive of the novelist's role as George Eliot conceived of
it: instead, self-confessedly coming to the novel with reluctance,
she devised a kind of novel that would allow her to explore those
questions in which she was interested and, equally importantly,
would not require her to undertake uncongenial duties.

   Hence, for instance, the limitations of her characterisation. As
Susannah Clapp has said, 'Like Fleur Talbot [in *Loitering with
Intent*], Mrs Spark does not usually "go in for motives": her
characters display themselves (as much of themselves as they
are going to display) by their actions'.[83] This makes for complex
and interesting plots but, very often, unsubtle, undeveloped
characters. But the novel of character, though it has had a long
run for its money, is not the only kind of fiction that can be
tolerated: there have always been exceptions (Bunyan's *Pilgrim's
Progress*, Hogg's *Justified Sinner*, Kafka's *The Trial*, Golding's *Lord
of the Flies*), and a novelist, like any creative artist, ought to be
allowed to define the terms within which she works. One has
the impression that Muriel Spark is not much interested in
people in their social roles and their relationship with others,
and this would indeed be a disabling indifference in a practitioner
of the novel of character. But no one who considers, for instance,
the portrait of Jean Taylor in *Memento Mori* or of Freddy Hamilton
in *The Mandelbaum Gate* could deny that she has the power to
present memorable characters when what is in question is not
'personal relationships' but spiritual health and the struggle to
realise the self.

   Another charge that has been brought against Muriel Spark
is that of what Alan Massie has referred to as 'the callousness,
the heartlessness, the despair of these novellas [from *The Public
Image* to *The Abbess of Crewe*], which is the world of Lear's heath,
or even Beckett'.[84] The case has been more fully stated by Patrick
Parrinder, who defines the problem as that of 'a witty, graceful
and highly intelligent writer who often fails to provide the
emotional satisfactions and to produce the sort of intellectual
conviction traditionally associated with novel-reading'. Parrinder's conclusion is that 'The high style of Muriel Spark is
lavished on a brutal and disillusioning world', and he confesses
himself 'troubled by her sensationalism, and her lack of compassion'.[85]

   The characteristics identified seem to belong, as Massie

concedes, to her later rather than her earlier work: 'despair' and 'brutality' are hardly characteristics of, say, *The Girls of Slender Means*, and *Memento Mori* is far from being a novel without compassion. The sensationalism is harder to deny and perhaps ought not to be denied: Muriel Spark is a moralist, not a sentimentalist or an idealist; she is unillusioned rather than disillusioned; and the 'brutal and disillusioning world' of her later fictions is no more so than the real world reflected in any day's newspaper. Earlier in his essay, Parrinder describes Muriel Spark as 'a genuinely disturbing writer – one who disturbs our deepest convictions and prejudices about novel-writing, and about more fundamental matters as well'. This seems to me to be praise of a high order, though in accomplishing her purpose of disturbing the peace (and *Not to Disturb* may be her most ironically effective title) she may also fail to provide what Parrinder calls 'the emotional satisfactions . . . traditionally associated with novel-reading'.

If so, so much the worse for traditional expectations. Muriel Spark is a novelist who sets out to 'make it new' in the long-established and, by the 1950s, slightly fatigued genre of the novel, and reading her can be an exhilarating as well as a disturbing experience. At a time when, at least in the British novel, many writers, even intelligent and inventive ones, have resorted to a drab and leaden prose, she uses English as if it were new-minted and her sharpness and subtlety of style are a constant source of surprise and delight. While so many postwar novelists write as if they were clothed in the 'austerity' garments of that unsensuous epoch, Muriel Spark seems to have retained some vision of splendour later satisfied, in the years of her prosperity, by her evident taste for expensive clothes and jewels.

All this is not to deny that there is a case to be made against Muriel Spark. Her world, though presented with an intensity that at times verges on the hypnotic, is not a large one. Some of her books – I would instance *Robinson* and *The Hothouse by the East River* – are relative failures. And there is, to my mind, an occasional touch of what might be called spiritual smugness: it may now and again cross the reader's mind that there is possibly something to be said for a writer's *not* having made her mind up on all the issues that really matter. There remains, however, a very substantial collective achievement of remarkable quality and originality. She acknowledges and owes few literary debts and belongs to no school, group or movement; there is no one quite like her, and one rereads her novels in the hope of coming a little closer to their meaning and in the certainty of repeated pleasure – as Fleur Talbot says at the end of *Loitering with Intent*, 'from there by the grace of God I go on my way rejoicing'.

Notes

1. Alan Massie, *Muriel Spark* (Edinburgh: Ramsey Head Press, 1979), p. 20.
2. Muriel Spark, 'What Images Return', in *Memoirs of a Modern Scotland*, ed. Karl Miller (London: Faber and Faber, 1970), pp. 151–2 (originally published in the *New Statesman* in 1962).
3. Ruth Whittaker, *The Faith and Fiction of Muriel Spark* (London: Macmillan, 1982), p. 18.
4. Derek Stanford, *Muriel Spark: A Biographical and Critical Study* (London: Centaur Press, 1963), p. 43.
5. Derek Stanford, *Inside the Forties: Literary Memoirs 1937–1957* (London: Sidgwick & Jackson, 1977), p. 152.
6. Stanford (1963), p. 28.
7. Ibid.
8. Stanford (1977), p. 184.
9. Muriel Spark and Derek Stanford, *Emily Brontë: Her Life and Work* (London: Peter Owen, 1960; repr. Arrow Books, 1985), pp. 11–12. The biographical sections of the volume are by Muriel Spark.
10. Stanford (1963), pp. 57–8.
11. Ibid., p. 59.
12. Muriel Spark, 'My Conversion', *Twentieth Century*, CLXX (Autumn 1961) 58–9.
13. Stanford (1977), p. 189.
14. 'My Conversion', pp. 59–60.
15. Ibid., p. 60.
16. Stanford (1963), p. 62.
17. 'My Conversion', p. 62.
18. Frank Kermode, 'The House of Fiction: Interviews with Seven English Novelists', *Partisan Review*, XXX (Spring 1963) 80.
19. *Daily Telegraph*, 25 September 1970, p. 15 (Muriel Spark was interviewed in London by Jean Scroggie).
20. Kermode, pp. 79–80.
21. Patricia Stubbs, *Muriel Spark*, 'Writers and their Work' series (Harlow: Longmans and British Council, 1973), pp. 5–6.
22. Massie, p. 21.
23. Alan Bold, *Muriel Spark*, 'Contemporary Writers' series (London: Methuen, 1986), p. 41.
24. Malcolm Bradbury, *Possibilities: Essays on the State of the Novel* (London: Oxford University Press, 1973), p. 248.

25. Frank Kermode, 'Sheerer Spark', *Listener*, 24 September 1970, p. 426.
26. Bold, p. 43.
27. Peter Kemp, *Muriel Spark*, 'Novelists and their World' series (London: Paul Elek, 1974), p. 37.
28. Whittaker, pp. 48–9.
29. Bold, p. 48; Kemp, pp. 34–5.
30. Kemp, p. 37.
31. Bold, pp. 53, 50, 49.
32. Stubbs, p. 8.
33. Massie, p. 30.
34. James Hogg, *The Private Memoirs and Confessions of a Justified Sinner, Written by Himself*, 'Oxford English Novels' series (London: Oxford University Press, 1970), pp. 124–5.
35. Massie, p. 31.
36. Cf. Muriel Spark's comments on marriage in 'My Conversion': 'It's a bit of a nuisance [for a Catholic] not being able to have a sex life if you are not married, but it has its advantages if you have a vocation, a mind obsessed with a certain subject or a job to do in life. It's not so easy for people less obsessed. The best thing then is to get married if you can. . . .' (p. 61)
37. Bold, pp. 59–62.
38. Kemp, pp. 59–70.
39. Whittaker, p. 62.
40. Francis Russell Hart, *The Scottish Novel: A Critical Survey* (London: John Murray, 1978), p. 302.
41. Massie, p. 48.
42. A. S. Byatt, 'Whittled and Spiky Art', *New Statesman*, 15 December 1967, p. 848.
43. Stubbs, pp. 24–5.
44. The point is made by Kemp in his fine discussion of this novel (pp. 84–96).
45. Kermode, 'Sheerer Spark', p. 426.
46. Ibid.
47. Whittaker, p. 78.
48. Kemp, p. 101.
49. Ibid., p. 104.
50. Whittaker, p. 70.
51. Stubbs, pp. 26–7.
52. Whittaker, p. 115.
53. Kemp, p. 115.
54. Ibid.
55. Bradbury, pp. 250–1.
56. As I was writing this chapter a psychiatrist was reported as saying, at a meeting of the British Association for the Advancement of Science, that 'many murder victims have personality disorders and seal their fate by provoking their killers' (*The Times*, 8 September 1988). An interviewer who talked to Muriel Spark in the year in which *The Driver's Seat* was published refers to the 'modern Swedish furniture' in her Rome apartment (*Daily Telegraph*, 25 September 1970, p. 15).
57. Kermode, 'Sheerer Spark', p. 426.

58. Bold, p. 94.
59. Kemp, p. 132.
60. Whittaker, p. 119.
61. Ibid., p. 131.
62. Bold, pp. 95–6.
63. Whittaker, p. 121.
64. Bold, pp. 96, 98.
65. Kemp, p. 141.
66. Ibid., pp. 141, 146, 157.
67. Whittaker, p. 103.
68. Ibid., pp. 105, 104.
69. Bold, pp. 99, 101.
70. Whittaker, pp. 82–3.
71. Ibid., p. 82.
72. Ibid., p. 87.
73. Bold, p. 110.
74. With Muriel Spark one ought never to take anything for granted, but in fact 30 June 1950 *was* a Friday. However, the date was not, strictly speaking, 'right in the middle of the twentieth century' (p. 200): that would presumably have been midnight on 31 December 1950/1 January 1951.
75. Whittaker, p. 121.
76. Bold, p. 114.
77. One of the sections of Proust's *A la recherche du temps perdu* is titled *A l'ombre des jeunes filles en fleurs*.
78. According to Derek Stanford, she had been commissioned by the publisher Frank Sheed to write a book on Job in the early 1950s; Stanford recalls her reading part of the introduction to him, but it seems never to have been finished. On 15 April 1955 Muriel Spark published in *The Church of England Newspaper* 'The Mystery of Job's Suffering', a substantial review of C. J. Jung's *Answer to Job* in an English translation. The essay suggests that 'The stumbling-block for most intelligent readers of *Job* is the epilogue'.
79. Bold, pp. 116–18.
80. There is also some self-quotation in this novel. A speaker on the BBC radio programme 'The Critics' singled out for praise, as an example of Muriel Spark's wit in *A Far Cry from Kensington*, the expression 'a rapacity for suffering'; the phrase is also used of Caroline Rose in *The Comforters* (Penguin edition, p. 38). Possibly a detailed search would yield further examples.
81. Professor Philip Thody tells me that the expression 'pisseur de copie' appears not to exist in French, though there is a slang expression 'un pisse-copie', meaning a hack-writer.
82. 'What Images Return', p. 152.
83. *London Review of Books*, 2 June 1988.
84. Massie, p. 76.
85. Patrick Parrinder, 'Muriel Spark and her Critics', *Critical Quarterly*, XXV (Summer 1983) 23–31.

Select Bibliography

MURIEL SPARK'S WRITINGS

NOVELS

The Comforters (1957
Robinson (1958)
Memento Mori (1959)
The Ballad of Peckham Rye (1960)
The Bachelors (1960)
The Prime of Miss Jean Brodie (1961)
The Girls of Slender Means (1963)
The Mandelbaum Gate (1965)
The Public Image (1968)
The Driver's Seat (1970)
Not to Disturb (1971)
The Hothouse by the East River (1973)
The Abbess of Crewe (1974)
The Takeover (1976)
Territorial Rights (1979)
Loitering with Intent (1981)
The Only Problem (1984)
A Far Cry from Kensington (1988)

SHORT STORIES

The Stories of Muriel Spark (USA edition, 1985; UK edition, 1987) contains stories that appeared earlier in *The Go-Away Bird and Other Stories* (1958), *Voices at Play* (1961), *Collected Stories I* (1967) and *Bang-Bang You're Dead and Other Stories* (1982). *Voices at Play* also contains the scripts of several radio plays.

POEMS

The Fanfarlo and Other Verse (1952)
Collected Poems I (1967)
Going Up To Sotheby's and Other Poems (1982)

BIOGRAPHY AND CRITICISM

(Edited with Derek Stanford) *Tribute to Wordsworth: A Miscellany of Opinions for the Centenary of the Poet's Death* (1950)

Child of Light: A Reassessment of Mary Wollstonecraft Shelley (1951)
(Edited, with introduction) *A Selection of Poems by Emily Brontë* (1952)
(Edited, with introduction) *The Brontë Letters* (1953)
(Edited with Derek Stanford) *Emily Brontë: Her Life and Work* (1953)
(Edited with Derek Stanford) *My Best Mary: Selected Letters of Mary Shelley* (1953)
John Masefield (1953)
(Edited with Derek Stanford) *Letters of John Henry Newman* (1957)

MISCELLANEOUS

Doctors of Philosophy (1963) (play)
The Very Fine Clock (1969) (children's book)

ARTICLES

Muriel Spark published a number of articles in the earlier part of her career, of which the most important are the following:
'The Religion of an Agnostic: A Sacramental View of the World in the Writings of Proust', *The Church of England Newspaper*, 27 November, 1953.
'The Mystery of Job's Suffering', *The Church of England Newspaper*, 15 April 1955.
'How I Became a Novelist', *John O'London's Weekly*, 1 December 1960.
'My Conversion', *Twentieth Century*, Autumn 1961.
'What Images Return' [recollections of Edinburgh], in *Memoirs of a Modern Scotland*, ed. Karl Miller (1970).

INTERVIEWS

Muriel Spark has given numerous interviews; some of those originally given on radio or television have been published in an abridged form or not at all. The following may be consulted by anyone interested in the *obiter dicta* of an artist who in recent years has increasingly preferred to let her works speak for themselves (the interviewer's name is given in parenthesis).
Queen, August 1961 (Elizabeth Jane Howard).
Sunday Times, 30 September 1962 (Joyce Emerson).
Partisan Review, Spring 1963 (Frank Kermode).
Observer Colour Supplement, 17 October 1965 (Mary Holland).
Guardian, 30 September 1970 (George Armstrong).
Listener, 24 September 1970 (Ian Gillham).
Daily Telegraph, 25 September 1970 (Jean Scroggie).
Observer Colour Supplement, 7 November 1971 (Philip Toynbee).
Sunday Express, 4 May 1973 (Graham Lord).
Listener, 28 November 1974.
Guardian, 8 November 1974 (Alex Hamilton).
Observer, 30 May 1976 (Lorna Sage).

CRITICISM OF MURIEL SPARK

BOOKS

The best of the eight books devoted to Muriel Spark are those by Peter Kemp and Ruth Whittaker. Kemp's *Muriel Spark* (1974) is often brilliantly perceptive and is extremely well written, but deals with the novels only as far as *The Hothouse by the East River*. Whittaker's *The Faith and Fiction of Muriel Spark* (1982) is thoroughly researched and more complete, lacking discussion only of *The Only Problem* and *A Far Cry from Kensington*. The other books (those by Stubbs and Malkoff are actually no more than pamphlets) are:

Alan Bold, *Muriel Spark* (1986).
Alan Bold (ed), *Muriel Spark: An Odd Capacity for Vision* (1984).
Karl Malkoff, *Muriel Spark* (1968).
Allan Massie, *Muriel Spark* (1979).
Derek Stanford, *Muriel Spark: A Biographical and Critical Study* (1963).
Patricia Stubbs, *Muriel Spark* (1973).

There is no biography of Muriel Spark, but Stanford's book listed above, supplemented by his somewhat franker account in *Inside the Forties: Literary Memoirs 1937–1957* (1977), provides some interesting material on her early career in London.

REVIEWS

Muriel Spark's books have been widely reviewed as they appeared, and some of these reviews are worth looking up. A number of the most interesting (by, for example, A. S. Byatt, Frank Kermode, Evelyn Waugh and Angus Wilson) are referred to in the notes. A lengthy list will be found in the bibliography of Ruth Whittaker's book.

Index